PLAYS BY
STUART SPENCER

D1594577

BROADWAY PLAY PUBLISHING INC
56 E 81st St., NY NY 10028-0202
212 772-8334 fax: 212 772-8358
http://www.BroadwayPlayPubl.com

First printing: March 2000
ISBN: 0-88145-169-X

Book design: Marie Donovan
Word processing: Microsoft Word for Windows
Typographic controls: Xerox Ventura Publisher 2.0 P E
Typeface: Palatino
Copy editing: Michele Travis
Printed on recycled acid-free paper and bound in the U S A

CONTENTS

ABOUT THE AUTHOR

In addition to the plays in the volume, Stuart Spencer is the author of numerous one-act and two-act plays, which have been produced both in New York at the Ensemble Studio Theater (where he is a member) and around the country. His play BLUE STARS is published in the Best American Short Plays of 1993-94. As an undergraduate, his play THE GOLDEN ROSE was designated "Best Play" at the American College Theater Festival, Midwest Region.

As a screenwriter, he has been commissioned to write films for Campbell Scott and for the director George Camarda. He has recently completed an original screenplay, *For You, Anything*.

Mr Spencer currently teaches playwriting in private classes, and formerly did so at the Ensemble Studio Theater Institute for Professional Training and the Young Playwrights Festival program that brings the art of playwriting into New York's inner city schools. He teaches dramaturgy and dramatic literature at Sarah Lawrence College, and at New York University.

He has served as a theater and film editor of Bomb Magazine, a quarterly magazine that publishes writing and art by, and interviews with, contemporary artists. His interview subjects include Robert Schenkkan, Campbell Scott, Joyce Carol Oates, John Ford Noonan, and Horton Foote.

Formerly Mr Spencer has held positions in the story editing department of C B S Films and the literary department of the Ensemble Studio Theater, where he served as Literary Manager for two years. In this latter capacity he helped to discover and cultivate new American writers and their plays, supervised and served as dramaturg for an ongoing series of readings, workshops, and major productions of the theater, and moderated the Playwrights Unit that included, at the time, such notable writers as Eduardo Machado and John Patrick Shanley.

He is a member of the Dramatists Guild and is a fellow of the Edward Albee Foundation.

For my mother

SUDDEN DEVOTION

SUDDEN DEVOTION was originally produced on 13 September 1994 at the Ensemble Studio Theater in a special workshop presentation. The cast and creative contributors were:

ROBBIE .... Chris Berger
HUGH, etc .... Kevin O'Keefe
NOAH .... Frank Raiter

Director .... Andrew Volkoff
Stage manager .... Scott Levy
Assistant stage manager .... Chris Shinn

My special thanks to all the above, who devoted themselves not only suddenly but completely in this labor of love, and to Judy Minor, who was so invaluable to me in writing the play.

CHARACTERS

ROBBIE
STAN
NOAH
HUGH
PETER
THE ESCORT

One actor plays the roles of STAN, HUGH, PETER, and the ESCORT. He should have some kind of simple but obvious device in his costuming that makes a clear distinction between his characters.

The play requires a very fluid sense of staging, as though it is all taking place in the mind of ROBBIE.

The time is the present.

...human intercourse...is seen to be haunted by a spectre. We cannot understand each other...we cannot reveal ourselves, even when we want to; what we call intimacy is only a makeshift; perfect knowledge is an illusion...We are people whose secret lives are invisible.

E M Forster

...just one look and then I knew
That all I longed for long ago was you.

Ira Gershwin

ACT ONE

(A Saturday afternoon. An apartment in Soho. Early spring. The late 1980s. A rainy day)

(We hear: distant street noises, the steady downpour of the rain, and a soaring, dreamy music.)

(Before us, a pale blue sky, rumpled, stretching from one side of the stage to the other. ROBBIE and STAN are asleep, utterly still.)

(The music fades as ROBBIE wakes up and turns to the audience.)

ROBBIE: Maybe we've been asleep for a hundred years.

Sometimes I think that's why
People wrote those fairy tales.
I think they woke up from a killer nap
And they looked around
And they thought to themselves
Have I been asleep for a century? Maybe I have.
Or maybe I'm still asleep and just dreaming.
I mean, how could they tell?
No clocks, no calendars
Just the great, slow turning
Of the stars and planets.

(ROBBIE turns back to STAN and wakes him up.)

ROBBIE: Good afternoon.

STAN: *(Sleepy)* Hi...

ROBBIE: We fell asleep.

STAN: We sure did.
  I feel like I've been sleeping forever.

ROBBIE: Maybe you have been. I'm going to make some coffee. You want some?

STAN: What time is it?

ROBBIE: Two thirty. Something like that.

STAN: *(He starts to get up.)* No, forget it, I don't have time. I've got an appointment with my agent.

Uh! I think I need another nap to recover from that first one. *(He gets up and begins dressing.)*

ROBBIE: It's raining out there. You're going to get soaked.

STAN: Maybe it'll wake me up. A little rain on the face. A little sweet cool rain.

(ROBBIE crosses to his tripod.)

STAN: Hey, what are you doing?

(ROBBIE snaps a picture of Stan dressing.)

ROBBIE: I'm just saving your posterior for posterity.

STAN: *(Laughing)* Well, knock it off.

(ROBBIE snaps another. STAN gets serious.)

STAN: I said knock it off.

ROBBIE: I'm capturing you in your wild state.

STAN: Come here.

ROBBIE: I'm just trying to do my job. I am a professional, after all.

STAN: Hello...

ROBBIE: What?

STAN: Come *here*.

(ROBBIE comes up close to him.)

STAN: Will you please relax?

(He kisses ROBBIE.)

ROBBIE: I like this, right there. *(He brushes with his finger the spot beneath STAN's nose.)*

STAN: Now let me get dressed. I'm late for my appointment.

ROBBIE: Is that all you care about? Seeing your agent? Making money?

STAN: Yeah, pretty much.

ROBBIE: Filthy lucre. Your mind is consumed by dollars.

STAN: You're trying to start an argument with me.

ROBBIE: You're an ambitious slut for money.

STAN: *(Correction:)* Prostitute for money. Sluts do it for free.

ROBBIE: What a beautiful vest. It's Versace, isn't it?

STAN: It's from the Gap.

ROBBIE: Well it's very nice anyway.

STAN: I've got to go. I'm sorry. *(He kisses* ROBBIE *and turns to go.)*

ROBBIE: Hey Steve. Don't you want to know when your proofs will be ready?

STAN: When will my proofs be ready?

ROBBIE: Next week.

STAN: I'll call you then. And my name isn't Steve.

ROBBIE: Stu.

STAN: Stan.

ROBBIE: Of course. Stan. Stan. God, what an idiot. Stan. Of course.

STAN: You know—my agent likes to choose my head shots. Why don't you send the proofs to him?

ROBBIE: Sure. No problem.

STAN: Thanks. And don't worry about my name—I can't remember yours either.

*(*STAN *exits. The lights change and* ROBBIE *addresses the audience.)*

ROBBIE: I hate when I do that.

I want to believe it so much—
That it's real—
That we've magically skipped over
All those tedious months and years of actually
Getting to know each other,
That suddenly we're just old, familiar lovers—
I want to believe that so much
That sometimes I just...make it up.

I end up forgetting which is the real world,
And which is the one I've only dreamed.

*(*NOAH *has entered, up stage of* ROBBIE. *He is blind. He carries a wet umbrella.)*

NOAH: Ahem.

*(*ROBBIE *turns around, surprised.)*

NOAH: I'm sorry. Please, finish your conversation.

ROBBIE: No, I was just... *(He looks back to the audience.)* ...I'll be right back... *(Back to* NOAH, *firmly)* ... I was talking to myself.

NOAH: Oh yes, of course. I know all about that. It gets worse when you're older. I sometimes have entire arguments with myself, doing both parts. *(Confidentially)* The trick is to give yourself the final word.

ROBBIE: Was there something I could do for you?

NOAH: This is a photography studio, isn't it?

ROBBIE: Yes.

NOAH: Perfect. That's what I want. To be photographed. Is that possible?

ROBBIE: Do you have an appointment?

NOAH: An appointment? Oh no—I'm afraid not. Do people make appointments?

ROBBIE: Normally, yes...

NOAH: Perhaps you could make an exception in my case because I'm so old and frail.

ROBBIE: As long as you put it that way.

NOAH: It's awfully kind of you. My name is Noah.

ROBBIE: Robbie.

NOAH: Shall I sit? Stand? Recline, perhaps?

ROBBIE: Oh sorry...here. The stool. *(He guides* NOAH *to it. He goes to his camera.)*

NOAH: You'll have to tell me what to do, of course. I'm not used to having my photograph taken. Although I suspect I have the knack for it.

ROBBIE: You just sit here, on the stool and be yourself. *(He begins taking pictures.)*

NOAH: What do you think of my face? Be honest.

ROBBIE: You have a very good face.

NOAH: Do I.

ROBBIE: Yes. Full of character. Good lines.

NOAH: What do you think of my nose?

ROBBIE: Very noble.

NOAH: You're flattering me.

ROBBIE: Not at all.

NOAH: Do you flatter all your clients?

ROBBIE: Never.

NOAH: I can smell flattery. It's honey on warm toast.

ROBBIE: Look towards me just a little.

NOAH: You don't believe me.

ROBBIE: Of course I do.

NOAH: I can smell all kinds of things. Memories for example. And desires. And regrets. I once smelled the regret of a young woman who had not visited her dying mother. It was the smell of mildew.

ROBBIE: I've heard a little Lysol does wonders.

NOAH: And there was a man once, middle aged and gone to fat, who longed for the beautiful young waitress who served him his coffee at the diner every morning. That smelled of unlacquered wood, freshly cut.

ROBBIE: Chin up, please.

NOAH: You think I'm kidding.

ROBBIE: That's too much.

NOAH: Well I'm not.

ROBBIE: Thaaaat's right.

NOAH: Now you take this studio of yours, for example. I detect the odor of old, rusty tin. Rusty tin on a rainy night. Unmistakable.

ROBBIE: And what does that mean?

NOAH: Rusty tin on a rainy night?
    Sorrow. Loneliness.

(ROBBIE *looks up from the camera.*)

NOAH: A great aching of the heart. *(pause)* Are you all right?

ROBBIE: I'm fine.

NOAH: Are you sure?

(ROBBIE *steps back from the camera.*)

ROBBIE: We're done, that's all.

NOAH: So soon?

ROBBIE: I've been shooting for nearly thirty minutes.

NOAH: It seemed like only a moment.

ROBBIE: Yes, people often say that.

NOAH: How strange. Well. I must be off then. When will it be ready?

ROBBIE: One week for the proof sheets.

NOAH: One week?

ROBBIE: I'm afraid that's how long it takes.

NOAH: Can't we speed that up a bit? I'm dying, you see.

ROBBIE: Oh...well, I could...I don't know—put in a special order.

NOAH: Could you?

ROBBIE: Yes.

NOAH: That would be so nice.

ROBBIE: How about Tuesday?

NOAH: Much better.

ROBBIE: Then I'll...uh...see you on Tuesday.

NOAH: I do hope so. Good bye.

ROBBIE: Here. *(He hands* NOAH *his umbrella.)* It's still raining.

NOAH: I detest the rain, don't you? *(He opens the umbrella.)* It smells like...well, just like *rain*.

(He exits. ROBBIE *turns to the audience.)*

ROBBIE: The next day
I'm on the way to the midtown lab.
I'm waiting for the walk light
When I look across to the opposite corner
And I see...

(Daylight. Traffic sounds. HUGH *enters in suit and tie.)*

ROBBIE: This *guy*.

*(*HUGH *notices* ROBBIE, *looks furtively at him and then looks away.* ROBBIE *stares him down until* HUGH *looks back. They share a brief moment of eye contact, then* ROBBIE *crosses to him.)*

ROBBIE: Got the time?

HUGH: Twelve-thirty. *(Long pause)* Yes, I do.

ROBBIE: My name is Robbie.

HUGH: Hugh.

ROBBIE: Me what?

HUGH: No—*Hugh*. That's my name. Hugh.

*(*ROBBIE *extends his hand.* HUGH *hesitates.)*

ROBBIE: It's just a handshake. Straight men do it all the time. Nobody will suspect a thing.

(They shake hands.)

HUGH: You do this a lot, I guess.

ROBBIE: Now and then. You?

HUGH: Not on my lunch hour.

ROBBIE: There's nothing to be nervous about. Just act like you know me.

HUGH: But I don't know you.

ROBBIE: But act like you do. Do you have a place?

HUGH: Me?

ROBBIE: Well, where were you planning on going?

HUGH: I figured you knew a place.

ROBBIE: I live downtown.

HUGH: I live uptown.

ROBBIE: We could get a hotel room.

HUGH: Really?

ROBBIE: Why not?

HUGH: Do people really do that?

ROBBIE: Are you kidding? We'll be lucky to find one free at this hour. We've got the walk sign.

HUGH: Wait.

ROBBIE: What?

HUGH: I can't do this.

ROBBIE: Relax, would you?

HUGH: Look, I'm sorry. I can't....

ROBBIE: I've got rubbers with me, if that's what you mean. I'm always safe.

HUGH: No, it's just....

ROBBIE: And I'm negative, if you're interested.

HUGH: No...I mean...yes, of course. That's great.

ROBBIE: And you?

HUGH: And me what?

ROBBIE: Are you negative?

HUGH: Well, yes.

ROBBIE: So what's the matter?

HUGH: Look, I go bars if I want this kind of thing to happen. I don't do it on my lunch hour on 45th and Madison. Can't we just...can't I just give you my number and we get together some other time?

ROBBIE: I hate doing that, trading numbers. It's too retarded.

HUGH: It's perfectly sensible.

ROBBIE: No, I mean retarded literally. As in slow.

HUGH: But I work in this neighborhood. I could be seen by people I work with. One of the partners, for instance.

ROBBIE: Right—they could also see you giving me your number.

HUGH: That's a little different.

ROBBIE: You've got an hour anyway, don't you? Give yourself a treat. Be daring. Live the fantasy.

HUGH: I'm just don't think it's prudent.

ROBBIE: Prudent? You don't think it's prudent?

HUGH: I'm giving you my number.

ROBBIE: I'm not taking it.

HUGH: I've got a card.

ROBBIE: I'm not taking it.

HUGH: Just take the card. Call me.

ROBBIE: I'm not taking it and I'm not calling you.

HUGH: Please?

ROBBIE: Sorry. I'll see you around. *(He starts to leave.)*

HUGH: Wait a minute. Wait...! *(He goes to* ROBBIE, *who has stopped.)* I like you. Obviously. But can't you understand that this is...it's out of context for me? It's unfamiliar. You are unfamiliar. I know nothing about you.

ROBBIE: And you know so much about those guys you pick up at bars, I suppose.

HUGH: I know their type, anyway.

ROBBIE: Their *type*? What's their type?

HUGH: *(Obviously...)* They go to bars.

ROBBIE: *(New approach)* Look, what do you think I am?

HUGH: What do you mean?

ROBBIE: You said you were nervous. What do you think I am?

HUGH: You certainly don't act nervous.

ROBBIE: Of course not. That wouldn't be as interesting, would it.

HUGH: That never occurred to me.

ROBBIE: Well, it's true. I'm nervous. And now you know something about me. Does that make you feel better?

HUGH: No.
  Yes.

ROBBIE: We've got the walk sign again.

HUGH: You're nuts. You know that?

ROBBIE: Yes.

HUGH: I mean, you're really nuts.

ROBBIE: Yes, and?

HUGH: And I guess I kind of like that.

(HUGH *exits.* ROBBIE *turns to the audience.*)

ROBBIE: The scene in the hotel room has been omitted.
  For reasons of good taste.

(A phone rings.)

ROBBIE: But later that evening...

(Lights up on HUGH, *who picks up the phone.)*

HUGH: Hello?

ROBBIE: That was nice today.

HUGH: Oh, hello.

ROBBIE: Hi.

HUGH: It was, yes. It was very nice.

ROBBIE: What are you doing now?

HUGH: I just got home from work.

ROBBIE: You want to come over?

HUGH: ...Well, uh, I don't know. I'm kind of tired.

ROBBIE: We could take a nap.

HUGH: Listen, what happened today was...well, great. But I don't want to
hurry anything.

ROBBIE: Hurry.

HUGH: As in fast.

ROBBIE: As in prudent.

HUGH: As in we could just go really slow.

ROBBIE: As in prudent.

HUGH: Well, that's all I'm prepared for at the moment.

ROBBIE: Okay—so do you want to come over?

HUGH: You're impossible.

ROBBIE: Just for dinner. You have to eat, don't you?

HUGH: I know what you're thinking. I'm some kind of uptight, uptown squarehead pain in the ass....

(In the following section, HUGH crosses until he ends up in ROBBIE's apartment.)

HUGH: ...but I just don't have a lot of practice at this kind of thing. I only came out a couple years ago and well, I have to be honest with you. Life is a little complicated at the moment.

ROBBIE: You have a boyfriend.

HUGH: No, no—

ROBBIE: You have a girlfriend.

HUGH: No, no—

ROBBIE: You have a wife. Tell me when I'm warm.

HUGH: I'm a lawyer. I work all the time.

ROBBIE: Oh, you mean it's not convenient.

HUGH: It's not that it's not convenient, it's....

ROBBIE: But it's not easy to accommodate your....

HUGH: Right, exactly—to accommodate my schedule.

ROBBIE: Your schedule. Of course. It's hard to find the time.

HUGH: Exactly.

ROBBIE: It wouldn't be prudent.

HUGH: You're making fun of me.

ROBBIE: Thanks for coming over. *(He touches HUGH.)*

HUGH: Look, I just have to say...

I'm not in a position right now. I'm working hard. And I'm good. I'm very good. I'm planning on making it happen. The career. I'm not prepared to devote the time to something...something more.

ROBBIE: I'm trying to think. Did I propose marriage and I'm just not remembering it?

HUGH: Of course not, no, but—

ROBBIE: Dinner. I asked you over for dinner.

HUGH: But you touched me.

ROBBIE: Yes?

HUGH: You touched me on the arm as if you were...

ROBBIE: Yes?

HUGH: One thing leads to another, that's all.

ROBBIE: Let me take your picture. *(He moves to the camera.)*

HUGH: My what?

ROBBIE: Your picture. Photograph. That's what I do.

HUGH: Oh, no. No, I don't think so.

ROBBIE: Oh please, it's just a picture. People pay me a lot of money to do this.

HUGH: But what do I do?

ROBBIE: You just go stand there. Right over there. That's right.

HUGH: But what do I *do*?

ROBBIE: Think about planetary motion. Think about all the planets, moving around the sun, all at the same time. Circling around the sun in this giant dance. All the planets. It would be a waltz, I think.

HUGH: A waltz.

ROBBIE: Yes—something grand, something elegant.

HUGH: All right.

ROBBIE: Can you do that?

HUGH: Sure. Let's see. A waltz.

ROBBIE: Have you got it?

HUGH: Yes, I think so.

ROBBIE: It's like meditation.

HUGH: Like what?

ROBBIE: Meditation. You focus on all those spinning orbs, floating in space—orchestrated but independent. So simple by themselves but impossibly complex as a group.

HUGH: Got it.

ROBBIE: That's the idea. Now think of that...and now look at me. Right to me. *(He starts taking pictures)* I get a lot of good pictures this way.

HUGH: It's kind of fun, isn't it.

ROBBIE: That's the idea.

HUGH: All those planets.

ROBBIE: Keep thinking.

HUGH: There goes Mercury. Whoosh!

(ROBBIE *goes on clicking.*)

And Saturn. Great, lumbering Saturn.

ROBBIE: That's right.
It's really a great way to see into a person. See what they're about. Get them thinking about something like that and the doors just open wide. They can't help it. They don't even know it's happening. The trick of taking a great photograph is to be able to see right into a person, to look into the inside. Deep inside.

HUGH: Okay.

ROBBIE: What?

HUGH: I just think that's enough.

ROBBIE: I'm not done.

HUGH: No, that's it. (*He walks away.*) I don't want to do this anymore.

ROBBIE: You want to see them when they're developed?

HUGH: Not really.

ROBBIE: Not even curious?

HUGH: I don't like pictures of myself.

ROBBIE: You've never seen these.

HUGH: Look, it was fun, okay? But I hate pictures of myself. I don't care if they're good or not. I hate them.
Maybe I'd better go now.

ROBBIE: There was a second there, today, in the hotel, when—I don't know—it all seemed to connect. For me, anyway. Or re-connect even. Like after a long separation.
I do that—in my head. I get that feeling. It happens without me wanting it to. A door opens and there's a whole world there and I want to step into it.
Sometimes, though, there is no other world there. Just an empty elevator shaft. But I step anyway, and down I go.
You'd think I'd learn to look first, wouldn't you. (*Moving on*) Well, I really *am* hungry.

HUGH: What I was thinking on the corner today was "Please."
"Please come here where I can talk to you. I can't come to you. I don't know why. I just can't. But please come to me. Please."
And you did. And I was glad about that. It was very...it was very very good. But like I said, I don't have a lot of experience here. I mean, my straight friends all go around dating and marrying and all that stuff and it looks very easy. But it isn't easy for me. It's like trying to read a book in a

foreign language. One word at a time. Very slow and very difficult.
   And, well...I'm actually not hungry. They give us dinner at the office when
we work late.

ROBBIE: Okay.

HUGH: And the thing is that I'm a little sore from this afternoon and I'm not
sure it's a good idea if we...

ROBBIE: We don't have to have sex.

HUGH: But I'm here now and I'd like to stay. Please. If that's okay. If you're
not thinking, *God, this guy just waffles incredibly.* I mean, if that doesn't turn
you off completely.

ROBBIE: It's fine. I like waffles.

(HUGH *smiles and extends his arms.*)

HUGH: "Please." That's what I was thinking.

(*As the lights fade,* ROBBIE *steps into another light and addresses the audience.*
HUGH *remains in his own light.*)

ROBBIE: And so he spends the night.
And the next.
And the next.
And every morning he says...

HUGH: I have to go home tonight, I'm running out of clean clothes.

ROBBIE: And every night he knocks at the door and says...

(NOAH *has appeared.*)

NOAH: Excuse me.

(ROBBIE *turns, surprised.* HUGH *disappears.*)

ROBBIE: *(To the audience)* That's not what he says.

NOAH: You were doing it again, weren't you.

ROBBIE: Yes.

NOAH: If you're going on like this now, it's going to be hell when you get
old.

ROBBIE: Come in.

NOAH: Are the proof sheets ready?

ROBBIE: Didn't we say Tuesday?

NOAH: Yes.

ROBBIE: This is Monday.

NOAH: I thought there was a chance they might be done early.

ROBBIE: Oh you did.

NOAH: Was I right?

ROBBIE: As a matter of fact, they came back today. *(He looks for the proof sheets.)*

NOAH: A person in my condition has to strike even if he isn't sure that the iron is hot.

ROBBIE: *(Produces a large envelope)* Here we are.

NOAH: What did you think of them?

ROBBIE: Honestly? I haven't had a chance to look at them.

(NOAH has taken out the proof sheets and takes a sniff.)

NOAH: Lots of good ones in this batch. *(Sniffing again)* Oh yes. *(To* ROBBIE*)* You're very good aren't you.

ROBBIE: I make a living.

NOAH: And I can see very well why. Well then. Which one?

ROBBIE: Which one what?

NOAH: Which one should I take? You decide. *(He thrusts the proofs at* ROBBIE.*)*

ROBBIE: Well, I'd need a little time.

NOAH: Ridiculous. Just point to one and we'll call it a deal.

ROBBIE: This is an art. The art of revealing the human soul. You can't just stab your finger at one picture and say "that's the one." It takes time.

NOAH: Time is something I don't have a great deal of.

ROBBIE: It's worth it—believe me. Take the time.

NOAH: That's very easy for you to say.

ROBBIE: If you hurry, you'll only end up with a picture of yourself that you don't like, and you'll never want anyone to see.

NOAH: But I've told you. I think they're lovely.

ROBBIE: All of them?

NOAH: Yes.

ROBBIE: All of them the same?

NOAH: Yes.

ROBBIE: What do you want it for? Maybe that will help us choose.

NOAH: *(As though it's obvious)* It's a record. That's all. Documentation. I was here.

ROBBIE: Yes, but what sort of qualities are you looking for?

NOAH: I don't know.

ROBBIE: You must have some idea.

NOAH: I want to be remembered. I want someone to look at the photograph and remember me and know who I was.

ROBBIE: *(Pause)* I think you should take them with you.

NOAH: What for?

ROBBIE: Take them home with you, live with them a bit. Smell them. For a week or so. Then we can get together again.

NOAH: A week or so.

ROBBIE: Yes.

NOAH: Meaning two weeks.

ROBBIE: Sure—that sounds good.

NOAH: Who do you think I am—Methuselah? Well, I suppose if I put my mind to it I ought to be able to last that long. I'll call you then. *(He turns to go.)*

ROBBIE: How do you know?

NOAH: Hm?

ROBBIE: How do you know you're dying?

NOAH: I can smell it, of course.

(NOAH exits and the lights change. ROBBIE turns to the audience.)

ROBBIE: And the time with Hugh slips past
With the strange, disorienting velocity
Of a dream.
But unlike a dream,
He is always there, real as the morning.

(HUGH has appeared, getting dressed.)

HUGH: I've got to borrow one of your shirts again.

ROBBIE: Hugh, I'm running out of shirts.

HUGH: Well, you've got nice shirts. How do I look?

ROBBIE: Very nice.

HUGH: Really?

ROBBIE: Yes.

HUGH: You really think so?

ROBBIE: Yes, I do.

HUGH: You're just saying that.

ROBBIE: You're wearing my shirt, my belt, and my shoes. Why shouldn't you look good?

HUGH: This is my belt.

ROBBIE: No, it's mine.

HUGH: Really?

ROBBIE: You've been wearing it for almost a month.

HUGH: Well, possession is nine tenths of the law, you know.

ROBBIE: I think you may be stealing my belt.

HUGH: Not stealing. Appropriating.

ROBBIE: I've got a better idea. Why don't you just move in with me?

HUGH: *(Laughing)* Right!

ROBBIE: Is that funny?

HUGH: You're such kidder!

ROBBIE: Well, you've been here every night for three weeks. At a certain point, moving in becomes a formality.

HUGH: I can't move in with you.

ROBBIE: Why not?

HUGH: Two reasons: number one, my mother. Number two, my father.

ROBBIE: Do you ever think you might come out to them?

HUGH: No.

ROBBIE: Never?

HUGH: That's right.

ROBBIE: You mean you're going to spend your whole life like this?

HUGH: Yes.

ROBBIE: You don't even have to think about it?

HUGH: Look, I simply prefer a scenario in which my parents die peacefully. If I tell them, I'm the one who dies. And believe me, not peacefully.

ROBBIE: I love you. *(Beat)* You don't need to respond to that if you don't want to.

HUGH: You don't even know me.

ROBBIE: Of course I do. I can read your thoughts. I'm tuned into your wave length.

HUGH: I have news for you...

ROBBIE: Wait a second, I'm picking up a signal.

HUGH: Robbie...

ROBBIE: *(In a "*HUGH *voice.")* "Gee I'd sure love to move into this place. Good southern exposure. High ceilings. Fabulous guy in residence. Plenty of clean shirts."

HUGH: *(Fighting a smile)* Could we just...please...give it some time? Please?

ROBBIE: Like how much?

HUGH: Like I don't know. Just time.

ROBBIE: Is that what you say to your all boyfriends? Let's wait a while and then we'll see?

HUGH: I've never had a boyfriend.

ROBBIE: I thought you...I mean I just assumed that...

HUGH: You know how busy I am. You know I work seventy hours a week, sometimes more.

ROBBIE: No, of course. It's just weird, thinking about it.

HUGH: And I never met anyone like you. I can't sleep without you, okay? But there's one thing.

ROBBIE: What?

HUGH: You and I are not boyfriends. I get nervous calling things by name. It's like I'm fourteen years old again. I don't want start ruining something by giving it a name. Or by moving in.

ROBBIE: Okay.

HUGH: Okay. *(Pause)* I'm late for work.

ROBBIE: I love my shirt.

HUGH: I love your shirt too. *(He kisses* ROBBIE.*)* I'll see you tonight. *(He exits.)*

(Lights change to a park. As ROBBIE *speaks to the audience,* NOAH *enters and sits on a park bench.)*

ROBBIE: Even in a dream,
There are moments of great clarity,
When you know you're dreaming.

Just as there are times in life
That are so palpable you can touch the moment itself.
(To NOAH*)* What do you dream about?

NOAH: Words.

ROBBIE: *Words?*

NOAH: Mysterious words. Like "red". Or "gold". Or "green". I dream a lot about "green". What is "green"?

ROBBIE: It's...really weird—I can't explain it.

NOAH: And "beautiful". That's another one. What does it mean for something to be "beautiful?"

ROBBIE: I don't think I can help you there either, Noah.

NOAH: Oh well...time to stop smelling the roses. Just because I suggested we meet in the park doesn't mean I don't want to get some work done. We're supposed to be looking at the proofs.

(ROBBIE *goes to him and takes a look at the proofs.*)

ROBBIE: What do you want people to see when they look at your picture?

NOAH: You already asked me this.

ROBBIE: No, I mean literally. What do you want people to get from it— what will they walk away with?

NOAH: Well, let me see. I fancy myself a man of nature. So, I'd say— the smell of freshly cut alfalfa, sweet with the early morning dew.

ROBBIE: But that's a smell. You have to give me something I can work with. People can't see the smell of freshly cut hay....

NOAH: Alfalfa.

ROBBIE: Alfalfa then...

NOAH: There's a difference.

ROBBIE: ...in a photograph.

NOAH: I can.

ROBBIE: Ordinary people.

NOAH: They could if they tried.

ROBBIE: Noah, really...

NOAH: *You* could, certainly.

ROBBIE: Noah, let's stick to the work.

NOAH: You could Robbie.

(ROBBIE *starts to speak.*)

NOAH: I'm telling you, you could.

ROBBIE: Smell things.

NOAH: Yes.

ROBBIE: As you do.

NOAH: Yes, of course.

ROBBIE: I don't think so.

NOAH: You've never tried.

ROBBIE: You're right. I haven't.

NOAH: Well?

ROBBIE: Oh stop...

NOAH: What are you, chicken?

ROBBIE: I'm olfactory challenged, okay?

NOAH: Touche!

(They smile, then....)

ROBBIE: Look, I need to get back for an appointment.

NOAH: So soon?

ROBBIE: I'm sorry. I've got a shoot at two o'clock. Why don't we meet again next week? I'll leave more time.

NOAH: All right.

ROBBIE: Look, I know you're in a rush, but...

NOAH: Actually, no. It's the strangest thing. Since I've begun to study the proof sheets, I seem to have a new lease on life. Things smell pretty good at the moment.

ROBBIE: Next week then.

NOAH: The park again?

ROBBIE: Yes.

NOAH: The park then. A week from today.

ROBBIE: One week.

ROBBIE & NOAH: Monday.

(NOAH exits as...)

(The lights rise on HUGH. He pushes an elevator button as ROBBIE joins him.)

HUGH: Where is this elevator?

ROBBIE: Hugh, I've got to tell you, I just don't know about this.

HUGH: *(Looking up at the floor indicator)* It's just sitting there.

ROBBIE: This whole summer share thing.

HUGH: Robbie, you've never even been to the Island. How would you know.

ROBBIE: I just don't think the Island is really my scene.

HUGH: Sometimes I think you're a latent heterosexual.

ROBBIE: It's that whole "Fags On The Beach" thing. The "Everywhere You Look Another Fag In His Calvin Klein Underwear In The Middle Of The Day" thing. I think it's kind of false.

HUGH: Robbie, this is where I go in the summer.

ROBBIE: Look, I'm sorry. I don't mean...I'm not talking about you, but....

HUGH: It's liberating. You get out there on Friday afternoon and everyone is settling into their house and going to tea dances. And night falls and there's that ocean breeze. And people are wandering up and down the walks. And you have dinner and do some Special K and go out dancing and don't come back until the sun is coming up over the ocean. And you wake up late and go to the beach and just lie there half asleep and think about nothing but the sun and the water.

And you're always slightly light headed, always the tiniest bit dizzy. It's the spell, cast by the Island itself. And you lose all track of time—is it Saturday afternoon? Or Sunday already? Have I been here all summer? Or is this only the beginning?

I lay on the beach one Labor Day weekend and I swore to myself it was only July. It *felt* like July. I was sure it was July. But the next day I was back in the office and it was September.

And you never once think "God, I wonder what those fucking straight people think about this," because there are no straight people. You're just living your life, the way you want to live it and there's nobody there to stare, or judge, or whatever.

I can't let go here like I can out there. You'd see a whole other side to me. We could know each other out there. Really know each other.

(The elevator arrives and the doors open. They get in and the doors close.)

ROBBIE: My parents have a place up in the Berkshires. We could go there on weekends.

HUGH: Oh wouldn't that be rich. You and I in Great Barrington, holding hands on the front porch. Your parents would be thrilled.

ROBBIE: My parents are very cool.

HUGH: I wonder how cool they're going to be when we're up at their summer cottage and they hear us in the room next door, humping.

ROBBIE: They'll be good little WASP parents and put in their earplugs.

(The elevator arrives again. The doors open and HUGH steps out.)

HUGH: Are you coming?

(ROBBIE *follows, reluctantly.*)

ROBBIE: It would be the real world, Hugh.

HUGH: Maybe I don't want the real world. Maybe I get the real world all day long every day and I don't want it every summer weekend when I'm trying to relax.

(*They stop.*)

HUGH: This is their door. (*Pause*) Look, I'm trying to take another step. Robbie, I hardly know you. You hardly know me. There's no time and if there is time, I'm too uptight in the city. Nobody at the law firm knows I'm gay. My parents don't know I'm gay. The people in my building don't know I'm gay. My dog doesn't know I'm gay. And it stops me, dead in my tracks. I can't open up, even when I want to.

ROBBIE: It doesn't have to be that way—nobody knowing.

HUGH: It is that way. Period. And it's going to stay that way for the foreseeable future. So I go someplace where people do know and everyone is just like me. And I like that. I'm comfortable with it.
     And if you come with me, you'll like it too because I'll be with you and you'll be with me and you'd better decide before we ring the doorbell.

(ROBBIE *turns to the audience.*)

ROBBIE: How can I say no?

(*The sound of a doorbell*)

ROBBIE: And so we open the door into another world.

(*Light change. The park bench. Day.* NOAH *is on the bench.*)

NOAH: I'll see you there, then.

ROBBIE: You have a place on the Island?

NOAH: Doesn't everyone?

ROBBIE: And you like it?

NOAH: Magic. Enchantment. You'll see.

(*Light change.* HUGH *is discovered on the top deck of a ferry boat. He beckons to* ROBBIE.)

HUGH: There! Can you see?! Right over there!

(ROBBIE *picks up his camera and crosses to* HUGH.)

ROBBIE: That's it?

HUGH: Yes.

ROBBIE: It looks like a sandbar, with trees.

HUGH: It is a sandbar.

ROBBIE: The way you described it, I was thinking a small volcano perhaps. Ar at least hidden lagoons and waterfalls. You know...enchanted. It looks so...small. So thin. Like a large wave could wash it away.

HUGH: You'll see. *(He puts his arm around* ROBBIE.*)* It casts a spell. It does something to people.

ROBBIE: Like what?

HUGH: *(Gives him a squeeze)* Like this.

*(*ROBBIE *notices* HUGH's *hand around his waist.)*

ROBBIE: *(Mock horror)* Oh my God. A Public Display of Affection.

HUGH: Well, we're on the island.

ROBBIE: We are?

HUGH: The ferry boat is officially considered island. And this is officially sanctioned island behavior. *(He kisses* ROBBIE.*)*

ROBBIE: Well, this probably isn't official island behavior. But I want you to have it anyway. *(He produces a ring.)*

HUGH: Robbie...

ROBBIE: I know, it's too much and it's too soon, but I'm going out on a limb here.

HUGH: Now don't go reading all kinds of symbolism into this. But I accept it. *(He takes the ring and puts it on and kisses* ROBBIE.*)*

ROBBIE: You're very unpredictable, you know that?

HUGH: And not at all prudent.
   Come on! We're there!

*(*HUGH *exits as the lights fade.* ROBBIE *turns to the audience.)*

ROBBIE: Unpredictable.
Little do I know.
We are only on the Island a day
And when I look for Hugh
I find he has just left the house,
Or is reportedly on his way back from the beach,
Or is simply not around.
And no one knows anything more.
And I begin to feel that old feeling,
Like somehow,
Maybe,
I've dreamed it all up.

(Lights up on the beach house. HUGH *enters, crossing in front of* ROBBIE.*)*

ROBBIE: I've been looking for you.

HUGH: Sorry—what's up?

ROBBIE: Nothing's up. I've just been looking for you all day.

HUGH: What for?

ROBBIE: Not for anything. I was just looking.

HUGH: Well here I am—but I've got to take a shower.

ROBBIE: Hugh.

HUGH: What?

ROBBIE: What's going on? What's up?

HUGH: I just really feel grungy. I want to rinse off.

ROBBIE: Where were you?

HUGH: I ran into someone, that's all.

ROBBIE: Like a friend?

HUGH: Yes. A friend. Okay? A friend. I ran into a friend. *(He starts to leave.)*

ROBBIE: Hugh.

*(*HUGH *stops.)*

ROBBIE: Are you going to tell me what the hell is going on?

HUGH: There is nothing going on!

ROBBIE: You disappear for two hours in the middle of the afternoon because you ran into some mysterious "friend" who doesn't have a name and you come back and you have to take a ...
...I think I just got it.

HUGH: Are we clear now?

ROBBIE: Who was it?

HUGH: Just somebody. I don't know who.

ROBBIE: What was his name?

HUGH: I didn't ask.

ROBBIE: Well...I...I don't know what to say.

HUGH: Then how about if we just say nothing.

ROBBIE: I don't get it. You just...went out and...did it? I mean, you just walked around until you...

HUGH: What are you asking about this for? Do you really want to know?

ROBBIE: I want to know!

HUGH: This is what I get for being honest.

ROBBIE: You weren't even going to tell me!

HUGH: I figured you just knew. Like I didn't have to spell it out for you.

ROBBIE: Well I didn't know.

HUGH: And I didn't think it was going to be such a big deal or I wouldn't have told you at all.

ROBBIE: Well it is a big deal!

HUGH: Okay! It is! Now I know that.

ROBBIE: I didn't think I had to say it.

HUGH: Obviously you did.

(Pause)

ROBBIE: Was it safe?

HUGH: Of course it was safe. What am I, an idiot?

ROBBIE: Yes, you're an idiot!

HUGH: Listen, this is the Island. This is what happens here. Everybody does it.

ROBBIE: I don't do it.

HUGH: Come on now. How do you think you met me?

ROBBIE: That was different.

HUGH: What was so different about it?

ROBBIE: We were both single at the time.

HUGH: And you made a big speech about how perfectly ordinary it was for us to go rent a hotel room in the middle of the day in midtown so we could do the deed.

ROBBIE: And you made a big speech about how you didn't do that kind of thing.

HUGH: Not in midtown, during the day.

ROBBIE: We were both single. That's the point.

HUGH: We are both still single, Robbie. I think I've made it pretty clear that's how I feel, haven't I?

ROBBIE: I'm in love with you.

HUGH: Oh Christ.

ROBBIE: I am.

HUGH: Would you stop?

ROBBIE: But I am.

HUGH: You use that like a weapon, you know that? "I'm in love with you." As if that gives you some sort of claim over me.

ROBBIE: I can't help what I feel.

HUGH: Listen, this is the package Robbie. You don't pick somebody up on the street corner one day and go to a hotel and then act surprised when that person turns out to be someone who likes to have sex with people. This should come as no surprise to you.

ROBBIE: Well I'm sorry but it does. I thought I knew you.

HUGH: Well you don't, okay? Love is not something that happens in a month, or in two months, or whatever. You're hot for me, maybe. You like me, we have fun together, I satisfy some need, but you are not in love.
  I think if you were really in love, it wouldn't make any difference. You'd sleep with other guys too and it wouldn't mean a thing.

ROBBIE: I don't want to sleep with anybody else.

HUGH: When you eat, do you only eat with me? When you go to a movie, do you only go with me? Am I the only person you kiss? The only one you love?

ROBBIE: Yes, as a matter of fact.

HUGH: You love your parents. You love your sister. You love Caroline and Jeff, you love your dog, you love your work.
  Your love is not exclusive, Robbie, no matter what you think. So why should we have a different standard for sex? Why should sex be the one thing that we can only do with each other? What kind of puritanical crap is that?

ROBBIE: Because that's how I feel about it.

HUGH: You want to fuck around, Robbie. Admit it.

ROBBIE: But I don't do it.

HUGH: But you *think* about it.

ROBBIE: Thinking about it isn't doing it!

HUGH: You're only angry because I go ahead and do what you want to be doing!

ROBBIE: Don't tell me what I want and what I don't want!

HUGH: You just told me yourself! You said you think about it! Well, so do I. I was out on the walk and I saw some guy and that was that.

ROBBIE: I don't want anybody else but you! You don't know that about me just like I didn't know this about you!

HUGH: Which only proves my point.

ROBBIE: What point?

HUGH: That you don't know me.

(Lights down on HUGH. ROBBIE *turns to the audience.)*

(Lights rise on NOAH, *on the beach under an umbrella.* ROBBIE *looks ready to explode.)*

NOAH: Go ahead...!

ROBBIE: Aaarrrgggghhhhhhhh!

NOAH: Better?

ROBBIE: Better.

NOAH: Sure?

ROBBIE: Yes.

NOAH: You're a good little screamer.

ROBBIE: You think you know a person but you put them down in another place and....

NOAH: You can never really know a person. You realize that, don't you?

ROBBIE: Of course you can.

NOAH: Not really. You might see them, touch them, *smell* them of course. But know each other? I don't think so. And certainly not in the time it takes for spring to turn to summer.

ROBBIE: I knew him instantly, from the moment we met.

NOAH: Impossible.

ROBBIE: It's not impossible! It happened!

NOAH: If you'd just give it some time.

ROBBIE: I don't have time!

NOAH: What's the great rush?

ROBBIE: You wouldn't understand.

NOAH: You made me understand about my portrait. About taking my time. Now I'm happy as a clam, just taking my time.

ROBBIE: This is different than your portrait.

NOAH: I don't think so.

ROBBIE: It's not the same.

NOAH: How so?

ROBBIE: *(Suddenly, a nasty tone)* It's just different, all right?!
I'm sorry.
When I was in college, I was in love with a boy. But he was straight.
He had a girlfriend. I mean, he knew I was gay, but I didn't want to ruin
things by saying...well, how I really felt.
Then we graduated and he had broken up with his girlfriend and we both
ended up in New York. I was still in love with him, but I realized I had to
get over him, start my life. So I had affairs with guys—who all reminded
me of him.
A few years went by and one day I got a call from the hospital that he was
there, sick with pneumonia. So I went to visit him. This was very early on
when they didn't know much and they were still losing people to
pneumonia. And he said, *Ever since I got to New York, I've been sleeping with
men. Lots of them. And I guess my luck didn't hold out.*
And I started to cry. And I held him in my arms and I said, *I love you.*
And he said *I love you too. I've always been in love with you,* he said. *I never
told you because at first, at college, I didn't know. And then after, in New York,
I thought that you didn't love me. And I couldn't bear the idea of saying that I
loved you, if you didn't love me.*
And the next day, he died.
And all I could think of was, if I had just said something, or done
something, right away. At the beginning. Just said, *I love you.* If I had just
done that, he would be alive now and we would be together.
There isn't time to wait. Not anymore. There's no time. People can be lost
forever.
I think I'd better get back now.
I'll see you tomorrow.

NOAH: Tomorrow?

ROBBIE: And bring the proofs.

NOAH: Tomorrow. *(He inhales deeply.)* Yes.

(Lights dim.)

END OF ACT ONE

ACT TWO

(ROBBIE *addresses the audience.*)

ROBBIE: And Hugh now begins to be an apparition,
A ghost—
Slowly turning more transparent
Until I can hardly see him at all.
Until I can hardly imagine his existence.

Sometimes I find myself calling out his name,
As if that alone would establish him as real.
If not present,
At least real.

Hugh!

(*Light change.* PETER *is discovered doing stretching exercises.* ROBBIE *enters, camera on his shoulder.*)

ROBBIE: (*Calling out*) Hugh?...Hugh! (*He sees* PETER.) Peter, have you seen Hugh?

PETER: He and Kevin went down to the grocery store.

(ROBBIE *starts to leave.*)

ROBBIE: Thanks.

PETER: Working?

ROBBIE: (*Stopping*) I'm sorry?

PETER: I said, are you working? Taking pictures?

ROBBIE: Yeah, I thought I might take a few of the Island. Just casual portraits, if people were willing.

PETER: Did I tell you I do some modelling?

ROBBIE: Really.

PETER: *Nude* modelling. I've got this photographer who likes my lines. That's what he says. My dancer's lines.

ROBBIE: Well, I do portraiture, mainly. And head shots.

PETER: Well portraiture is a kind of nudity, isn't it?

(ROBBIE *is unconvinced.*)

PETER: I mean, the face is nude, after all. There's nothing on it. Just bare flesh. *(He winces in pain.) Oooo!*

ROBBIE: What's wrong?

PETER: Nothing. I pulled a muscle the other day. I'm just stretching it out. You don't mind giving me a hand, do you?

ROBBIE: No—sure.

PETER: Just sort of massage right here. Yeah. That's right. Not too hard. *(Pause)* So how about it?

ROBBIE: *(Warily)* How about what?

PETER: Didn't Hugh tell you?

ROBBIE: Tell me what?

PETER: He thought you might want to do some pictures of me.

ROBBIE: Hugh said that?

PETER: He mentioned it, in passing.

ROBBIE: Oh. Well. Sure, all right.

PETER: Yes?

ROBBIE: Yes, why not?

PETER: You're sure.

ROBBIE: Yes.

PETER: How do you want me?

ROBBIE: I think...just keep doing what you're doing.

PETER: Stretching?

ROBBIE: Yes. We'll keep it informal. Natural.

PETER: Natural. All right.

(ROBBIE begins to photograph him.)

(PETER has hit a particular pose.)

ROBBIE: That's very nice.

PETER: Like this?

ROBBIE: Yes, right there. Hold that.

PETER: I'm holding, baby.

ROBBIE: And maybe take your left arm and...no your other left. That's right. Now just...just place it slightly to the side, like this. No, the other way. So it looks natural. No, that's too much. Here...if you put this arm here and this arm here, then you can sort of...(*He kisses* PETER.) I can't believe I just did that. I'm sorry.

PETER: It's all right.

ROBBIE: I don't know what I was thinking.

PETER: It doesn't mean anything. It's just the island. It's just the way it is out here.

(ROBBIE *kisses* PETER *again.*)

ROBBIE: When I met you in the city, that day that Hugh and I came over to meet you and the other guys. I didn't have the slightest interest in you. It was like...you were just one other guy. But then, ever since we've been on the Island, it's been very different, somehow.

PETER: Uh-huh.

ROBBIE: It's all a little confusing, but it's like I somehow know you in a completely different way. Or I just know you, period. Which I don't, of course, but...

PETER: What does that mean?

ROBBIE: What does what mean?

PETER: What does it mean when you know someone?

ROBBIE: It means you know them. You know about them. You know who they are. You know what they do, what they think, how they feel. You understand them.

PETER: Is that what it means?

ROBBIE: Doesn't it?

PETER: I don't know. I never knew what it meant—"I know you."

(*They kiss again.* ROBBIE *offers his hand to* PETER.)

ROBBIE: Come on. Let's just go.

(PETER *takes his hand and the lights change.* ROBBIE, *to the audience.*)

ROBBIE: And we go.
And in a moment,
Suddenly,
It's over.
And it's funny—
I don't feel bad.
I only feel
Nothing.

(*Lights up on* PETER *behind* ROBBIE.)

PETER: Hey. *(Pause)* Hey. *(He comes up behind* ROBBIE *and puts his arms around him.)* How about once more?

ROBBIE: I think I'd better get going.

PETER: Where are you going?

ROBBIE: Just...the pictures. I was going to take some shots.

PETER: All right.

ROBBIE: Peter.

PETER: Yeah.

ROBBIE: That was weird.

PETER: Was it? Why?

ROBBIE: Because I don't even know you.

PETER: I thought you did know me.

ROBBIE: Yes, of course I know you but...well, maybe that's why it was weird.

PETER: I see.

ROBBIE: And because of Hugh.

PETER: What about me?

ROBBIE: Hugh. Your friend, Hugh. My lover.

PETER: I wouldn't worry about that.

ROBBIE: I know you wouldn't worry about it. You don't have to worry about it. It's me that has to worry about it

PETER: No you don't.

ROBBIE: I think I do.

PETER: Hugh knows all about it. Why do you think he and Kevin didn't come back from the grocery store? If they went to the grocery store at all. Which is doubtful, considering I did all the grocery shopping yesterday.

ROBBIE: Oh. I see.

PETER: He knew it was going to happen. I imagine he figured—why not get it over with now. Release the tension. Enjoy the rest of the summer. I think he sort of felt like you needed a little push. This is the island. It really doesn't mean anything here. Nothing means anything.

(Lights fade on PETER. ROBBIE, *to the audience.)*

ROBBIE: And very quickly,
More quickly than I would like,
I come to believe he is right about that.
Nothing means anything.

(Lights rise on NOAH, *on the beach.* NOAH *is dancing to an upbeat, jazzy number.)*

NOAH: Robbie!

ROBBIE: Noah?!

NOAH: Come on! You try it!

ROBBIE: Right out here on the beach?!

NOAH: Come, come!

ROBBIE: *(Going to him)* I was never very good at dancing.

NOAH: This is the perfect dance for you, then. You make it up as you go along.

*(*NOAH *does a step and* ROBBIE *follows. This goes on for a moment.)*

NOAH: How are you doing?

ROBBIE: Great.

NOAH: Do we look silly?

ROBBIE: We certainly do.

NOAH: The Island casts its spell and we must do its bidding.
   We dance at the moment of decision. Only two left to choose from. Either this...or this. *(He holds two proofs in his hands.)* This one is a strong contender. Full-bodied.

ROBBIE: *(Still dancing)* It's the Dance Of The Seven Proof Sheets.

NOAH: A piercing lemony scent of surprise.

ROBBIE: The Dance Of Making Up Your Mind.

NOAH: Robbie...

ROBBIE: The Dance of My Life Is A Mess But I Don't Care!!!

NOAH: Robbie... Are you all right?

*(*ROBBIE *goes to* NOAH, *still dancing.)*

ROBBIE: I'm very all right.
   So, you think this is a contender?

NOAH: As I said, the piercing lemony scent of surprise.

ROBBIE: Very nice. Spontaneity.

NOAH: Exactly. But then we have the other...

ROBBIE: Also a good one.

NOAH: An element of mystery, I'd say.

ROBBIE: Sort of elusive. Ephemeral.

NOAH: The aroma of a fine, chalky powder.

ROBBIE: Something hard to grasp about it.

NOAH: Precisely.

(Pause)

ROBBIE: This is the one.

NOAH: Do you think?

ROBBIE: Absolutely.

NOAH: We've done it then. We've found my portrait.

ROBBIE: I'll have it printed next week.

NOAH: Only one print, though.

ROBBIE: All right.

NOAH: There must be only one. And then you destroy the negatives and the proofs.

ROBBIE: Yes, all right.

NOAH: It must be the only document of me. The unique photograph. *(Inhaling)* A fine, chalky powder.

(Light change. ROBBIE, to the audience.)

ROBBIE: So the summer passes,
And I become another person.
Easily,
Effortlessly,
I become another Hugh.
I disappear for an hour or two,
Unexplained.
I come home at sunrise,
Exhausted.

I take a lot of showers.

September arrives,
And with it
The final weekend of the summer.
We are both bored and silly,
Sitting in the house on Saturday afternoon
And for a moment, everything seems right...

(Lights up on HUGH. He is seated, a magazine in his hand. He is giggling. ROBBIE joins him.)

HUGH: I don't *believe* these personal ads.

ROBBIE: Oh my God.

(They giggle together.)

ROBBIE: Now, do you really believe that? Fourteen inches?

HUGH: Maybe he means his shoe size.

ROBBIE: Worse!

HUGH: And then of course we have the escort services. *(He flips to the next page.)*

ROBBIE: Oh, I hate those!

HUGH: Golden Boy Services. Young beautiful boys eager to serve.

ROBBIE: Stop, stop!

HUGH: Dream Guys. Totally Engaged.

ROBBIE: I wonder what *that* means.

HUGH: It means he does whatever you want. He is whatever you want him to be.

ROBBIE: You mean he's like you. You're everything I'd ever want.

HUGH: *(Back to the magazine)* Taboo. Young exotic demi-gods. Wow. Look at this one. He's gorgeous!

ROBBIE: Okay, he's gorgeous. So what.

HUGH: Nothing. I'm just saying.

ROBBIE: You're just saying what.

HUGH: I'm just saying he's gorgeous and they take credit cards.

ROBBIE: That's disgusting.

HUGH: And the price is really very reasonable. It would be kind of fun, wouldn't it? For both of us, I mean. We could split the cost.

ROBBIE: Hugh.

HUGH: What?

ROBBIE: You're trying to provoke me.

HUGH: No I'm not.

ROBBIE: You're deliberately pushing a button to see how I'll react.

HUGH: No I'm not. It just sounds like fun to have one of these guys. Can you imagine? Whatever I want him to be?

ROBBIE: I can't deal with this. *(He gets up.)*

HUGH: Where are you going?

ROBBIE: Don't you know how ridiculous this is? People our age do not hire hustlers.

HUGH: That's just it. Better to do it now, when I don't have to. When I'm old, it'd be pathetic. Anyway he's an escort, not a hustler. It's very high class.

ROBBIE: Right.

HUGH: Robbie, look at him for God's sake.

ROBBIE: I already looked.

HUGH: And you don't understand.

ROBBIE: That's right.

HUGH: You think he's gorgeous. Now admit it.

ROBBIE: You've taken away our relationship. You've taken away what I used to laughingly refer to as my self-worth. Would it be all right if you left me with my own taste in men? I know what I like and this is not it.
  Please don't do this.

HUGH: I suppose you'd rather I went out and picked up a trick.

ROBBIE: They've been good enough up until now.

HUGH: You've got to learn to loosen up.

ROBBIE: I don't want to loosen up any more than I already have. I don't even want to loosen up that much!

HUGH: Well, nobody's making you do anything, Robbie, so if you don't want to, just stop. Nobody said you had to fuck that guy while I was at the beach last weekend.
  He left his underwear in the bathroom.

ROBBIE: That was different.

HUGH: Different from what? Different from the trick you did two weeks ago right outside the disco in the bushes? Peter and I saw you leave with him. Was it different from that?

ROBBIE: They weren't hustlers! They were within the rules! Your rules!

HUGH: You like to think you can act just like your straight friends, but it doesn't work, Robbie. They've had practice—years of it. And they've got the whole world in back of them saying, yes. *Go do that. Go on that date. Get involved with that person. Get married.* Well you and I don't have that and we never will. And I'm sick of having to live by their codes and their expectations when I don't get anything in return from it. So while I'm here on the Island, fuck you and fuck them. I'm doing what I want!

ROBBIE: *You look at me, Hugh!* What the hell is going on in there?! You're my boyfriend!

HUGH: You know I hate that word!

ROBBIE: Who cares about the word! You're my toaster oven. Okay? You're my clock radio! We are what we are, Hugh. You can't deny it by denying the word!

You are not the person who would do something like this. *You are not that person!*

HUGH: I think I'll have him at nine tonight. Maybe it would be better if you weren't here. I'm saying that for your own good.

ROBBIE: You don't give a God damn about my own good! You have no idea what my own good is! You don't have a clue about who I am, or how I feel about things, or what I might want! Because if you did, you wouldn't be doing this!

HUGH: Robbie, I hate to say this, but that's exactly what I've been trying to tell you all along. I don't know. I admit it. You won't. You'd rather live in some fantasy world. And that's the whole problem. *(He waits a moment, then exits.)*

ROBBIE: I'll be right back. *(He exits. A pause, then from off stage...)* Arrrrggghhhh!

(The lights change to a sunset glow. We are on the deck. Sound of the ocean. NOAH *and* ROBBIE *enter.)*

NOAH: What is it this time?

ROBBIE: He's crazy! Over the edge! Down the shaft!

NOAH: All right, now wait a minute.

ROBBIE: My own good! He actually said that—my own good!

NOAH: Just wait, now slow down.

ROBBIE: Toaster oven! Okay?!

NOAH: Toaster oven?!

ROBBIE: Does that make him happy?!

NOAH: Toaster oven!? Robbie—wait!

*(*ROBBIE *is finally quiet.)*

NOAH: Now tell me. Tell me all of it.

ROBBIE: I don't even know where to start.

NOAH: Try once upon a time.

ROBBIE: Once upon a time?

NOAH: Once upon a time...

ROBBIE: Once upon a time, a long time ago—well not that long really, but it seems like forever—in this hotel room, in midtown, I felt so close to him. As if I knew every thought in his head, every flicker of emotion, no matter how subtle, how remote. Just by looking into his eyes, I knew.

And now after all this time, I feel like I should know him better, or at least as well. But everyday I say to myself, who is this man? Why don't I know him? I look into his eyes and I see...his eyes. I learn something about him—some habit, some secret—and it just confuses me.

The more I know, the less I know.

(The "sky" has been slowly changing from dusk to night as they speak. Slowly, a wide banner of stars is appearing against a deep black sky.)

ROBBIE: I just want to be together. To be *with* him.

NOAH: Be together *again*, you mean. *(Reminding him)* Hotel room. Midtown. To recreate that first sudden moment when you were joined, as if by magic.

ROBBIE: All I want is a chance to know him.

NOAH: Well if you want my advice, the trick is not to look into his eyes. Look at the sunset, both of you together, and if nothing else, for one moment, you can both know the sun. In this life, that's as close as we get to each other.
(He holds ROBBIE's face in his hands.)
You're in a magic place, Robbie. Let the magic do its work. It will take you where you have to go.

Now good night. It's an old man's bed time. *(He exits.)*

(THE ESCORT enters out of the shadows on the opposite side of the stage.)

ESCORT: Excuse me.

(ROBBIE turns around, surprised.)

ESCORT: Sorry. I didn't mean to walk in on you like this but no one answered at the door. I'm early for my appointment. I'm from the service.

ROBBIE: Really?

ESCORT: You know what I'm talking about, right? The service? I mean, I don't have to explain.

ROBBIE: You're an escort.

ESCORT: That's right.

ROBBIE: You escort people places.

ESCORT: That's right.

ROBBIE: "Places they've only dreamed of." Or at least that's what the advertisement says.

ESCORT: Is that what it says?

ROBBIE: You don't read your own press?

ESCORT: I'm afraid not.

ROBBIE: "He makes your dreams come true."

ESCORT: That sounds about right.

ROBBIE: You sound very sure of your abilities.

ESCORT: Give me a chance, I could prove myself.

ROBBIE: I don't think so. Not me.

ESCORT: You don't think I could do it.

ROBBIE: Frankly? No.

ESCORT: You haven't given me a chance. Go ahead, try me.

ROBBIE: All right. A lover.

ESCORT: You want a lover.

ROBBIE: That's right.

ESCORT: That could be arranged.

ROBBIE: Look, thank you very much. I appreciate the attention. But I'm afraid your appointment isn't here. He's down at a tea dance, getting properly trashed for the evening ahead. So let me suggest that you find a good magazine to read and wait for him to come back.

ESCORT: I can't do that.

ROBBIE: Why not?

ESCORT: My schedule. I had to schedule another appointment at midnight in the city. So I've got to be out of here by ten o'clock. *(He checks his watch.)* One hour.

ROBBIE: And then you go? Just like that?

ESCORT: I'm afraid so. It's a job, after all.

ROBBIE: Well, I know, but he'll be very disappointed.

ESCORT: I thought that maybe I could interest you in some business— since I have the time anyway.

ROBBIE: Thanks but no thanks.

ESCORT: It's not the money, is it?

ROBBIE: Not exactly.

ESCORT: Because we don't have to make it for money.

ROBBIE: I thought you said "business."

ESCORT: I did.

ROBBIE: Could you interest me in some "business" is what you said.

ESCORT: Jargon.

ROBBIE: Really?

ESCORT: That's what we say. Interest you in some "business?" Just a matter of language. Force of habit.

ROBBIE: So it wouldn't be for money.

ESCORT: No.

ROBBIE: Then what?

ESCORT: I just want to, that's all.

ROBBIE: That would make you very unusual, wouldn't it? Or am I mistaken?

ESCORT: Unusual how?

ROBBIE: What I've heard about you—about men in your line of work—what I've heard is that if somebody wants you, they have to come and get you. And pay for it. Always. Isn't that right?

ESCORT: This is an unusual circumstance.

ROBBIE: What's so unusual about it?

ESCORT: Lots of things.

ROBBIE: Like what?

(THE ESCORT *crosses to* ROBBIE *and kisses him. It lasts for a few moments, then* ROBBIE *tries to gently tug himself away.*)

ROBBIE: Wait, wait...

ESCORT: What?

ROBBIE: Hugh wouldn't like this.

ESCORT: How do you know what I'd like?

ROBBIE: No, Hugh wouldn't like it. Hugh. My lover.

ESCORT: I thought you said you didn't have a lover.

ROBBIE: Not exactly. I said I wished I had one. There's a difference.

ESCORT: So you have a lover, but you don't—at the same time.

ROBBIE: It doesn't make sense, I know.

ESCORT: But it does. He hired me, didn't he? That explains things fairly well.

(*He moves to* ROBBIE, *but* ROBBIE *backs away.*)

ROBBIE: I can't. I'm sorry.

ESCORT: I've got rubbers with me, if that's what you mean. I'm always safe.

ROBBIE: No, it's just....

ESCORT: And I'm negative, if you're interested.

ROBBIE: No...I mean...yes, of course I'm interested but....

ESCORT: Then what?

ROBBIE: It's just too fast, that's all. One second I'm standing here all alone, the next second we're...I don't know. I'm uncomfortable.

ESCORT: But you wanted to.

ROBBIE: Yes, of course, I...

ESCORT: You're attracted to me.

ROBBIE: Yes, of course, but...

ESCORT: Aren't you?

ROBBIE: Yes.

ESCORT: Then what?

(ROBBIE *can't answer.*)

ESCORT: I like you.

ROBBIE: You just happen to like me.

ESCORT: Yes.

ROBBIE: Just by coincidence.

ESCORT: That's right.

ROBBIE: You just happened to walk in here and found that you liked me.

ESCORT: Is there something wrong with that?

ROBBIE: Of course n-...

ESCORT: Am I not allowed, for some reason? A person of my profession— is that supposed to be beyond my capabilities?

ROBBIE: But how do you even know? You don't even know me.

ESCORT: It makes you nervous, doesn't it.

ROBBIE: Yes. It does. It makes me nervous.

ESCORT: That someone might just see you and know you and know what you're all about.

ROBBIE: Yes.

ESCORT: Don't you think it makes me nervous too? Don't you think that scares me?
   Be scared with me. Let's be scared together.

(ROBBIE *goes to* THE ESCORT. *They embrace and kiss.*)

(*In that same moment, there is a sound—a chord, or a ping, or a snapping noise—and the lights change suddenly.*)

(*Stars and moonlight appear. They are on the deck.*)

ROBBIE: How did we...?

ESCORT: How did we what?

ROBBIE: How did we get out here?

ESCORT: (*Smiles*) Magic. We flew.

ROBBIE: No, now wait, we...we were just on the deck and now we're on the beach.

ESCORT: Yes.

ROBBIE: I'm feeling dizzy.

ESCORT: Maybe it's the tide.

ROBBIE: The tide?

ESCORT: Pulling at you. It's coming in now. You can hear the waves. They make a different sound.

ROBBIE: How would the tide make me dizzy?

ESCORT: Pulling at you. Turning your head around.

ROBBIE: The tide doesn't do that. The tide doesn't pull at you. It's the moon that pulls at the tide.

ESCORT: That was nice before.

ROBBIE: It was, yes. It was very nice.

ESCORT: The way you make love. It's beautiful. You really communicate. (*To* ROBBIE'*s crotch.*) Hey—you listening to me?
   How about once more? Out here. On the beach.

ROBBIE: Listen, it was...well, great. But I don't want to hurry anything.

ESCORT: Hurry.

ROBBIE: As in fast.

ESCORT: You still think I'm going to send you a bill—is that it?

ROBBIE: No, no of course not. Are you?

ESCORT: (*Laughs*) Robbie, you're too much.

ROBBIE: But...

ESCORT: I want you.

ROBBIE: I want you too, but...I don't know. Stop looking at me.

ESCORT: Why?

ROBBIE: I'm trying to think. I can't think with you looking at me.

ESCORT: Why not?

ROBBIE: Because I can't concentrate.

ESCORT: *(Sees the camera nearby)* Let me take your picture.

ROBBIE: Oh, no. It's too dark.

ESCORT: No it isn't!

ROBBIE: No, I really don't think so.

ESCORT: Just go stand there. Right over there. I do a little photography in my spare time—just amateur stuff. Still, I'm pretty good.
    That's right. *(He has the camera and begins snapping.)*

ROBBIE: What do you want me to do?

ESCORT: Surrender to the camera. Look right at me. I want your true essence.

ROBBIE: Listen, I think that's enough. I don't like pictures of myself anyway. *(He moves away.)*

ESCORT: Robbie, what's wrong?

ROBBIE: I think you should go. This is making me crazy.

ESCORT: I knew the moment I walked out onto the deck and saw you. It was instant. You felt it too. I know you did. The moment when we knew both our lives would change. It's that feeling that we know each other. From long ago. That we've been separated for the longest time and now we've found each other again. And I knew my life would change. That you would change my life. And I knew you felt the same way about me. Why do you have to deny that? It's true isn't it? *(No response)* In that case, I'd better go.

ROBBIE: Stay until morning, then.

ESCORT: You're sure?

ROBBIE: Yes. Please. Please stay.

(ROBBIE opens his arms and THE ESCORT goes to him.)

(Again, a sudden light change accompanied by the Sound.)

(Bright daylight. The beach. THE ESCORT strips off his shirt as if he getting ready to go into the water.)

ESCORT: Come on, let's go in! The water looks great!

ROBBIE: *(To the audience, utterly baffled)* It keeps happening!

ESCORT: What's the matter with you? *(He has retrieved a towel and is looking ready for a swim.)* Robbie?

(ROBBIE snaps to THE ESCORT's attention.)

ROBBIE: Yes!?

ESCORT: You wanted to use my towel.

ROBBIE: Oh. Right.

ESCORT: Are you all right?

ROBBIE: What do you mean?

ESCORT: You look so, I don't know—stunned.

ROBBIE: I think I need to get out of the sun for awhile.

ESCORT: Are you having one of those moments?

ROBBIE: Yeah—I think I am.

ESCORT: Here, sit down.

ROBBIE: No, that's all right. I'm fine now.

ESCORT: Are you sure, Boobie?

ROBBIE: *Boobie?*

ESCORT: Boobie.

ROBBIE: What's Boobie?

ESCORT: I thought you liked it when I called you that.

ROBBIE: *Boobie?*

ESCORT: You know, I've been thinking. Would it be all right if I moved my stuff in with you?

ROBBIE: You are kidding, aren't you?

ESCORT: Well, I've been here every night for three weeks.

ROBBIE: You can't move in with me.

ESCORT: Why not?

ROBBIE: For one thing, what about Hugh?

ESCORT: What do you mean? You kicked him out.

ROBBIE: But it's so soon.

(THE ESCORT turns away.)

ROBBIE: What?

ESCORT: I guess I'm not used to this.

ROBBIE: To what?

ESCORT: It sounds like I'm bragging, I know, but...well, usually this is the other way around. Men have always wanted me. They've paid for me. And now that it's the other way around, I'm not sure what to do.
   I love you, Robbie.
   You don't have to say anything. I'm just letting you know.

ROBBIE: But you don't even know me.

ESCORT: Of course I do. I can even read your thoughts. I'm tuned into your wave length.

ROBBIE: I wish you'd stop saying things like that.

ESCORT: Things like what?

ROBBIE: *(To the audience)* He's plagiarizing my life! *(To* THE ESCORT.*)* Familiar things.

ESCORT: What do you mean?

ROBBIE: Could we just...please...give it some time? Please? I never met anyone like you. You're very...open. Which I like. But please...

ESCORT: All right. Okay. Time.

ROBBIE: Yes, exactly. Time.

*(*THE ESCORT *kisses* ROBBIE.*)*

ESCORT: I'll see you in the water.

*(*THE ESCORT *goes to* ROBBIE, *kisses him and turns to go. As he does so...)*

(The sudden light change and the Sound—this time with a slight variation.)

(A sunset glow. Still the beach. THE ESCORT *"re-enters.")*

ROBBIE: Oh God...

ESCORT: You like watching the sunset, don't you. You know what I like? Watching the sunset in your eyes.
   Are you ready to go?

ROBBIE: Where are we going?

ESCORT: Did you forget? We're going to meet my parents.

ROBBIE: Oh God, I don't know if I'm ready for this.

ESCORT: They're very cool. They'll like you.

ROBBIE: Do they know about us?

ESCORT: Of course. I've told them everything.

ROBBIE: Do they know about you?

ESCORT: Of course they do.

ROBBIE: I mean you. What you do.

ESCORT: That's all over now, Robbie. You've seen to that.

ROBBIE: Look, it's not that I don't want to meet your parents, but can't we wait a little bit? I mean, I've heard all about them and I know we're supposed to meet them. But I don't feel I'm quite ready.

ESCORT: My parents are another world. The real world. And I want to take you there.

ROBBIE: You always say you want to know me. But you won't ever do anything that might let that happen.

ROBBIE: Yes...

ESCORT: Isn't that true?

ROBBIE: Well...

ESCORT: Isn't it?
  Let it happen, Robbie.

(They embrace.)

(Light change and the Sound. The Ferry Boat.)

ESCORT: There! Can you see?! The mainland!
  This probably isn't the best time. But I want you to have this anyway.
  (He produces a ring.)

ROBBIE: What is that?

ESCORT: I know, it's too much and it's too soon, but I'm going out on a limb here.

ROBBIE: What does that mean?

ESCORT: I love you, Robbie.

(He holds out the ring to ROBBIE.*)*

ROBBIE: What are you doing? *(Pushes the ring away)* No, really, I can't.

ESCORT: Why not?

ROBBIE: I can't accept that.

ESCORT: You don't love me?

ROBBIE: I hardly know you.

ESCORT: But I want you to have it.

ROBBIE: Just put it away, would you? This is ridiculous.

ESCORT: I don't see anything ridiculous about it.

ROBBIE: It's too much.

ESCORT: What's too much about it?

ROBBIE: It's not the way I feel. Not yet, anyway.

ESCORT: Well, when? When are you finally going to feel something?

ROBBIE: When you give me the room to do it!

ESCORT: When haven't I given you room? That's all I ever do is give you room!

ROBBIE: Not enough!

ESCORT: Then why do you keep coming back to me?

ROBBIE: I like you. I'm attracted to you. But I don't know you and I can't know you when you keep pressing your face up against mine. Step back a little bit!

ESCORT: You want me with my face pressed up. That's exactly what you like!

ROBBIE: Says who?

ESCORT: Says you! You say it with everything you do in your life! And you know it!

ROBBIE: I don't know what you're talking about.

ESCORT: You take this ring!

ROBBIE: I don't even know your name!

ESCORT: You wanted it—now take the fucking ring!

ROBBIE: I just realized—I don't even know your name!

ESCORT: Here!

(He thrusts it at ROBBIE. ROBBIE *pushes it away.)*

ROBBIE: Get away!

(They struggle. ROBBIE *falls.)*

(Sudden light change and the Sound—this time more final sounding.)

(Night. The deck. The banner of stars again.)

(The two are silent for a moment, out of breath from their struggle.)

ESCORT: What the hell is your problem, Mister? I thought you said that was what you wanted.

ROBBIE: Where are we...?

ESCORT: I happen to be good at this, you know. I happen to know what I'm doing. People pay me a lot of money for this, and I don't need some jerk off like you giving me a hard time.

ROBBIE: What are you talking about?

ESCORT: I'm talking about when you ask for something from a professional, don't be so surprised if you get it. It's ten o'clock. Your time is up. You pissed away your hour. Better luck next time. *(He starts to go.)*

ROBBIE: Wait a second!

ESCORT: *(Stopping, impatient)* What?

ROBBIE: It wasn't real.

ESCORT: It was as real as you made it. It was as real as the feelings you supposedly have for some bogus boyfriend who calls up and hires me for the evening.

ROBBIE: There is nothing bogus about Hugh and me!

ESCORT: I would have had you too. Just a little bit longer and I would have done you. The one thing you wished for in all the world. "I wish I had a lover."

ROBBIE: Not like that!

ESCORT: Well if you're going to get particular about how, that's your problem. By the way: Jack. Now you know my name. *(He exits.)*

(NOAH enters. He carries what seems to be a rolled piece of paper in his hand.

NOAH: They come and go, don't they? And when they're gone, they're gone. That's the Island.

ROBBIE: I thought you'd gone home to bed.

NOAH: I did. I went home. And suddenly the air was heavy with the smell of clean linen, fresh from the iron.
    You don't smell it, do you?

ROBBIE: No, I'm afraid not.

NOAH: You could, you know, if you tried.

ROBBIE: Me?

NOAH: Yes.

ROBBIE: *(Skeptical)* No.

NOAH: Oh yes. I'm sure you could.

ROBBIE: Really?

NOAH: I think you're ready.

ROBBIE: All right.

NOAH: You'll try?

ROBBIE: Yes.

NOAH: Then we begin.
   Don't put your nose in the air. And you can leave your eyes open. Or close them, I don't care. Just don't do anything special. In fact, don't do anything at all. Just be here with me. And let the aroma come to you. Let it find you.

ROBBIE: Let it find me.

NOAH: That's right. Stay very still and let it do the work. Give it a little time to discover you and before you know it...

ROBBIE: There.

NOAH: Yes?

ROBBIE: I smell it.

NOAH: Freshly laundered linen.

ROBBIE: Yes. Very faint. Just a trace. No—now it's gone.

NOAH: Wait a moment. Relax. Let it find you again.

ROBBIE: Yes. There it is. Stronger now.

NOAH: Yes?

ROBBIE: Like clean, cold water and soap. Like a hot iron on fabric.

NOAH: That's it.

ROBBIE: Like a newly made bed.

NOAH: Yes.

ROBBIE: Like folded white shirts.

NOAH: Exactly.

ROBBIE: It seems very near.

NOAH: It is near.

ROBBIE: As though I could touch it.

NOAH: You can. *(He lifts his hand up in front of* ROBBIE.*)* Go ahead. Touch.

*(*ROBBIE *takes the hand and lifts it to his nose.)*

ROBBIE: It's you.
   What does it mean? What does linen mean?

NOAH: It means that young men aren't the only ones dying these days. Old men still die too. We don't even need a special reason. We just do it. I've smelled it before, on others. This time it's for me.

(ROBBIE *starts.*)

NOAH: Not tonight. Not tomorrow. But the thing approaches.

ROBBIE: You don't know—not for sure.

NOAH: I always told you I was in a hurry. You never believed me. You were too much in a hurry yourself to notice. *(He hands over the rolled paper. It is his portrait.)* Here. I want you to have the photograph.

ROBBIE: You're not going anywhere.

NOAH: It's not as if I haven't told you before, Robbie. I said it from the very beginning.

ROBBIE: Keep the picture. Just...keep it.

(NOAH *sets the envelope down on the ground.*)

NOAH: Let the rain wash over it. Let the sun bleach it out until there's nothing left of it.

ROBBIE: Look, I don't know why you're talking like this.

NOAH: Because I'm dying.

ROBBIE: Go, take it. Hang it back up in your bedroom. You're going to be fine.
   Go home. Take your picture and go home.

NOAH: You won't keep it for me, then.

ROBBIE: No.

NOAH: I wish you would.

ROBBIE: It's ridiculous. Me keeping it. It's yours.

NOAH: Not when I'm dead.

ROBBIE: Would you stop saying that!

NOAH: It's true Robbie.

ROBBIE: You don't know that!

NOAH: Have I ever been wrong before?

ROBBIE: You're wrong now!

NOAH: I'm right, I'm afraid.

ROBBIE: You're wrong!

NOAH: But Robbie...

ROBBIE: You're wrong!

NOAH: But I've smelled it!

ROBBIE: Keep the picture!

NOAH: Good-bye.

ROBBIE: Take it with you!

NOAH: Good bye.

ROBBIE: I love you! *(He seizes* NOAH *and wraps him in an embrace.)* I love you! Don't go away! I love you!

NOAH: I love you too, Robbie.

ROBBIE: You and I...we're in the same place. We smell the same scents, touch the same cloth, know the same thing.

NOAH: Yes. And isn't it beautiful? But the season is over, Robbie. So let me go now.

ROBBIE: Will you sleep?

NOAH: Yes.

ROBBIE: You could stay here.

NOAH: No.

ROBBIE: All right.

NOAH: You understand, don't you.

ROBBIE: I think so, yes.

NOAH: Good bye Robbie.

ROBBIE: Good night.

NOAH: Good night. *(He starts to go.)*

ROBBIE: Noah? I'll remember you.

*(*NOAH *exits.)*

*(*ROBBIE, *to the audience.)*

ROBBIE: I remain on the deck all night
Until the sun rises in the morning,
And it is only then
That Hugh returns.

(Light change. Morning. Still the deck. HUGH *enters and sprawls onto the ground.)*

ROBBIE: I fell asleep.

HUGH: Out here?

ROBBIE: Yes.

HUGH: I never hooked up with that guy last night.

ROBBIE: No?

HUGH: I stood him up, so I just stayed out and danced my ass off. How about some sleep.

ROBBIE: I'm not tired.

HUGH: Come on. I'm taking you inside.

ROBBIE: Not yet.

HUGH: Robbie, let me take care of you.

ROBBIE: I really don't want you to.

HUGH: You don't know what you want. You're exhausted.

ROBBIE: I want to stay and watch the sunrise. I like the light.

HUGH: The sun rises every morning.

ROBBIE: I want to watch the sunrise.

(Pause)

HUGH: You're pissed off at me.

ROBBIE: I just want some time to think.

HUGH: You think too much, that's what I think.

ROBBIE: Why don't you go to bed.

HUGH: You know why.

ROBBIE: I don't have any idea.

HUGH: Let's not play this game, okay?

ROBBIE: I really don't.

HUGH: You know why I don't just to bed.

ROBBIE: I don't know!

HUGH: Well, you used to know.

ROBBIE: Well, I don't know now.

HUGH: Well, you used to.

ROBBIE: The point is that I don't know. And I know that I don't know. And I don't pretend that I do know. That's the point. You have always claimed that I know nothing about you and now I admit it, all right? I know nothing. I don't know you. I don't know the first thing about you.
   Just go to bed, and I'll be out here and everything will be fine.

HUGH: Because I can't sleep without you, Robbie. You know that. *(Quickly, before* ROBBIE *can protest.)* All right, you don't know it. You used to, but you don't. But now you do.

(He draws up next to ROBBIE *so they are both looking out across the water.)*

HUGH: It's our last day. We have to pack up this afternoon. Back to the city for the winter.

ROBBIE: And then what? When we're back in the city?

HUGH: Robbie, what happened to you last night? Did something happen? Something happened.

ROBBIE: I don't want to try anymore, Hugh.

HUGH: What do you mean?

ROBBIE: I mean I don't want to try. I just can't try. I want you. But I can't try.

HUGH: Look at me.

ROBBIE: I don't want to look at you.

HUGH: Is it over then? Is that what you're saying? Robbie, are you breaking up with me?

ROBBIE: I just don't want to think about you right now. I want to look at the sun.

HUGH: It's not up yet.

ROBBIE: Yes it is—right there.

*(*HUGH *looks.)*

ROBBIE: In the haze. It's blurry, but it's there.
   Do you see it? Hugh? Do you see it?

(The lights and an adagio fade.)

END OF PLAY

RESIDENT ALIEN

ORIGINAL PRODUCTION

RESIDENT ALIEN was first produced by the Actors Theater of Louisville as part of the 22nd Annual Humana Festival of New American Plays, opening on 24 February 1998. The cast and creative contributors were:

MICHAEL . . . . William McNulty
PRISCILLA . . . . Carolyn Swift
RAY . . . . Brad Bellamy
THE ALIEN . . . . V Craig Heidenreich
THE SHERIFF . . . . Brian Keeler
BILLY . . . . Corey Thomas Logsdon

Director . . . . Judy Minor
Scenic design . . . . .Paul Owen
Costume design . . . . Nanzi Adzima
Lighting design . . . . Amy Appleyard
Sound design . . . . .Martin R Desjardins
Properties design . . . . Ron Riall
Stage manager . . . . .Juliet Horn
Assistant stage manager . . . . Charles M Turner III
Dramaturg . . . . .Michael Bigelow Dixon
Casting . . . . .Laura Richin Casting

CHARACTERS & SETTING

MICHAEL
PRISCILLA
RAY
THE ALIEN
THE SHERIFF
BILLY

All the characters are in their thirties, except BILLY, *who is about twelve.*

The stage setting should be minimal, fluid enough that the scenes can change easily and quickly.

ACT ONE

Scene One

(A farmhouse in Wisconsin. Late at night)

(On stage are MICHAEL *and* PRISCILLA *and* RAY. MICHAEL *sits in a chair.* PRISCILLA *and* RAY *circle around him.)*

MICHAEL: He wanted to go to the quarry. I said, "No, Billy, it's too close to bedtime." He said, "Come on, Dad. I want to see the sunset. It's summer. I don't have to get up for school."
     So I said, "Fine. But don't tell your mother."
     So we're walking through the woods, and it's already dark in there, even though the sky is still blue. And we get to that clearing—you know, where the trail heads off to the left there? And there was this light. Above, and behind us. Then it started to move towards us—this light—and we ran back down the trail, but it followed us.
     Then we saw it, right in front of us, on the ground. The light changed color and focused, like a narrow beam, pointing right at Billy. And Billy walked towards it, like a trance. But I was frozen in place. I couldn't move! And I yelled, "No! Take me! Take me!"
     And then...it was gone. One second, it was there. The next...nothing. And I was alone.
     At least I thought I was alone. They left someone. One of their own. He said, "We borrowed your friend. Don't worry. He'll be fine."

*(*PRISCILLA *walks up to him, confronting him.)*

PRISCILLA: Bullshit.

RAY: Okay, okay! Now hold on here. Okay Mike, so—that's all just fine. So, where is he now?

MICHAEL: I just told you, he's in the ship.

RAY: Not Billy—this guy they left. This alien.

PRISCILLA: Why are you asking him that?!

RAY: Because maybe we could talk to him.

PRISCILLA: Ray, there is no little green man.

RAY: Let's just hear the guy out once. Okay Mike, if they left someone, then where is he?

MICHAEL: I...I don't know. He left. He's not here.

RAY: He left? Where did he go?

MICHAEL: He didn't say. He said not to look for him.

RAY: And you didn't, I suppose.

MICHAEL: I'm not going to do anything he said not to. They have Billy.

RAY: But if he knows where Billy is ...

MICHAEL: He's in a spaceship!

PRISCILLA: Fine. We're calling the sheriff.

MICHAEL: Go ahead. Call the sheriff. It's not going to do any good.

RAY: *(To* PRISCILLA*)* He's right about that. If it's aliens, there's not much Hank's going to be able to do.

PRISCILLA: Ray.

MICHAEL: They took him away and he's not coming back until they decide.

PRISCILLA: Michael, you have bullshitted me once too often / / and you're not going to do it again...

MICHAEL: *(Overlapping at //)* Bullshat.

PRISCILLA: What?!

MICHAEL: "Bullshat" would be correct.

PRISCILLA: *(To* RAY, *suddenly at a loss)* You see what I'm dealing with?!

MICHAEL: You're a literate woman, Priscilla. I don't know why you pretend you're not.

PRISCILLA: You are not dragging me into a fight about the past tense of shit. No! I'm sorry! I refuse!

RAY: All right now Mike. Come on here. You don't expect us to really believe this.

MICHAEL: It's not a question of believing. When something happens to you—when it happens present tense, first person—then it's not like you either believe or you don't believe. It's just a matter of what happened to you. If you're in a car accident and you break your left arm, you don't go around afterwards saying, "Now I believe in car accidents." You just say, "I was in an accident. That's what happened to me."

PRISCILLA: You have a history, you know. It wouldn't be the first time you made things up, invented stories, imagined things that aren't true.

MICHAEL: I never "imagined" things!

PRISCILLA: You displayed an inability to distinguish between reality and fantasy! The shrink said that, not me!

MICHAEL: I was there! I saw it!

PRISCILLA: Oh yes, you always concocted stories, Michael, but at least it was always something original!

MICHAEL: Priscilla, this happened!

PRISCILLA: I'll take you into court if I have to.

MICHAEL: You do what you have to do. You always did.

PRISCILLA: You've taken advantage of my good nature too many times, Michael! I am Billy's legal custodian. Your visitation rights are all spelled out.

MICHAEL: I can't help what the people in spaceships do!

RAY: Okay, okay. Listen you two. It's time to saw this off. I got to get up and go fishing early.

PRISCILLA: You're not going fishing, mister.

RAY: I told Roger I was going to meet him up at Machickanee Flowage.

PRISCILLA: *(To* MICHAEL*)* If my son isn't on my doorstep first thing tomorrow morning, I'm calling the sheriff's office and I'm going to have you arrested. Is that clear? So you'd better go back out to the quarry, stick out your thumb, flag down that spaceship, and get them to beam Billy back down to earth before his mother throws one hell of an interplanetary fit. *(She exits.)*

MICHAEL: They don't beam people. That's T V.

RAY: See if you can't bring the kid back quick this time, eh Mike? They're really bitin' up to the Flowage. *(He exits.)*

(The door to the laundry opens and THE ALIEN *enters. He has a slightly greenish tinge to his skin.)*

ALIEN: Which one were you married to?

(Lights out.)

Scene Two

(The same, somewhat later, still night. MICHAEL *has fallen asleep, his head on the table. The* ALIEN *sits at the table, struggling with a book.* MICHAEL *wakes up with a start.)*

ALIEN: Hi.

MICHAEL: You're really here.

ALIEN: Yes.

MICHAEL: I thought maybe I was just dreaming.

(He rubs his eyes and checks his watch. He was sleeping longer than he thought.)

ALIEN: Sleep must be very boring.

MICHAEL: Actually it can be quite interesting.

ALIEN: Pretty slow going from this end. You do it a lot?

MICHAEL: Every night.

ALIEN: Wow. Sure wish you had a T V.

MICHAEL: Well I don't. I threw it out.

ALIEN: Bummer.

MICHAEL: *(Referring to the book)* What're you reading?

ALIEN: It's yours. Kierkegaard. I hope you don't mind.

MICHAEL: How do you like it?

ALIEN: I'm still working on the first sentence, actually. *(He reads.)* "If there were no eternal consciousness in a man, if at the bottom of everything there were only a wild ferment, a power that twisting in dark passions produced everything great or inconsequential; if an unfathomable, insatiable emptiness lay hid beneath everything, what would life be but despair?"
    Now what does that mean, exactly?

MICHAEL: It means there has to be something else.

ALIEN: Expand.

MICHAEL: Something other than mere passion, mere animalistic drive. Life is not only the wolf howling at the moon without consciousness. Life has meaning. Humanity has thought. We are aware, we're sentient. We endow the world with meaning through thought. We try to understand the nature of our own howl.

ALIEN: I see. *(He closes the book and hands it to MICHAEL.)* I guess I like more of a story.

MICHAEL: *(He takes the book and goes to the window.)* It's almost daylight.

ALIEN: Yes.

MICHAEL: They'll be back soon.

ALIEN: They will?

MICHAEL: You said they'd be back this morning.

ALIEN: Did I?

MICHAEL: Wait a minute. They won't be back this morning? Billy's not on his way home?

ALIEN: I'm sorry if you misunderstood / / but I...

MICHAEL: *(Overlapping at //)* Nobody misunderstood! You said they'd be back by sunrise!

ALIEN: I said 'they always come back by sunrise.' I didn't say this particular sunrise ?

MICHAEL: I trusted you!

ALIEN: Don't worry. It's all for a good cause. And they'd never hurt a soul.

MICHAEL: How do I know that?

ALIEN: How do you know he's not having a great time up there? He might be.

MICHAEL: Well, how much longer?

ALIEN: I don't know.

MICHAEL: Are we talking days? Weeks? Months? What?!

ALIEN: Oh days, days. At the very most, a week. Or two.

MICHAEL: Just tell me the truth. This is my son we're talking about!

ALIEN: Well I don't know. That's the truth. Sometimes it's short, sometimes it's long. But they always put the people back where they came from.

MICHAEL: Always?

ALIEN: Always.

MICHAEL: Really?

ALIEN: Almost certainly.

MICHAEL: I'm going back to the clearing.

ALIEN: Please don't do that.

MICHAEL: Why shouldn't I?

ALIEN: I worry about you.

MICHAEL: I can take care of myself.

ALIEN: You're upset. When people are upset they do things they don't mean to do.

MICHAEL: How would you know? What do you know about people? You said you'd never seen any people before me.

ALIEN: I said I never saw any humans. People I've seen all over the galaxy.

MICHAEL: Well, I am a people and I have to find my son.

ALIEN: I know, but believe me, he's not at the clearing. Not even close. Now please, won't you sit down?

(MICHAEL *resists for a moment, but finally gives in.*)

ALIEN: Here. Drink your coffee.

(MICHAEL *stares into his coffee.*)

MICHAEL: It's cold.

ALIEN: You don't like cold coffee?

MICHAEL: No.

ALIEN: Boy, things sure are different down here. See, to wake up in the morning we drink martinis—steaming hot. But we drink our coffee cold, at night, when we want to party up.

MICHAEL: Down.

ALIEN: What?

MICHAEL: I think you mean party down.

ALIEN: You see? Cultural exchange. I love it! Mind if I smoke? (*He takes out cigarettes and lights one.*) Smoking helps control our libido.

MICHAEL: What's wrong with your libido?

ALIEN: Nothing wrong with it. It's incredibly high, that's all. Wait a second, I forgot—you like to distinguish between gender here, don't you.

MICHAEL: Well, yes.

ALIEN: See, we don't do that.

MICHAEL: You sleep with anyone?

ALIEN: Not anyone. But somebody attractive, like yourself...

(MICHAEL *flashes him a worried look.*)

ALIEN: Relax, I'm smoking. It's fine.

MICHAEL: Could you just tell me one thing?

ALIEN: Of course.

MICHAEL: Why did you take him?

ALIEN: We prefer the term 'borrow'.

MICHAEL: Oh right. I feel so secure about my only son when you say you only "borrowed" him. My compliments to your language experts. They must be up on their George Orwell.

ALIEN: George Orwell. *1984.* Good movie.

MICHAEL: It's also a book.

ALIEN: Yeah, but once you see the movie, it sort of spoils it.

MICHAEL: The question is: why?

ALIEN: I think I lost you.

MICHAEL: Why did you take him?

ALIEN: Borrow.

MICHAEL: Why?

ALIEN: Some obscure test to investigate some statistical aberration in some previous test that is part of some longer, on-going survey that's part of some endless study of some tiny little behavioral quirk. You know what these people are like: inquisitive, eager little minds. So annoying.

MICHAEL: Billy's not in any danger, is he?

ALIEN: Well that's a relative question. No pun intended.

(MICHAEL *doesn't crack a smile.*)

ALIEN: See, you're his relative and...never mind.

MICHAEL: Is he in danger?

ALIEN: Let me put it this way. He walks to school everyday, right?

MICHAEL: Yes.

ALIEN: Is that dangerous?

MICHAEL: Of course not.

ALIEN: Well, but—getting hit by an automobile or accosted by some random lunatic. You never know.

MICHAEL: Well there's some danger just in getting up in the morning.

ALIEN: There you go. Couldn't say it any better.

MICHAEL: You don't even know what's going on up there, do you.

ALIEN: Hey, I'm support team, okay? It's some kind of very fancy I Q test. I don't know the details.

MICHAEL: I thought you were an advanced race.

ALIEN: Advanced race, yes. But I work in the kitchen. I'm a...what's your word again? Carboy?

MICHAEL: Busboy.

ALIEN: Right...

MICHAEL: If you're a busboy, then what are you doing here?

ALIEN: Shore leave.

MICHAEL: This is insane.

ALIEN: Look, it's been a long time stacking plates and filling water glasses, okay? I need a break. And from everything I hear, earth sounds like a pretty good time. Best T V shows, best C Ds, best magazines, best movies, best snacks. Best everything! I was hoping you could give me a sort of a tour—I'd love to do an outlet mall, for instance.

MICHAEL: Is this common? "Shore leave"?

ALIEN: No—strictly forbidden. They'd kill me if they found out.

MICHAEL: Kill you?!

ALIEN: Well, no. But they might make me scrub pots all the way to the next solar system.

MICHAEL: So you know nothing.

ALIEN: No.

MICHAEL: You're useless.

ALIEN: I think I have a few skills.

MICHAEL: But essentially, you're useless. My boy is kidnapped and....

ALIEN: Borrowed.

MICHAEL: My boy is kidnapped, and you're just here to "party up".

ALIEN: Down.

MICHAEL: I know.

ALIEN: Listen, I could have just walked off and left you back at the clearing, but I happen to be warmhearted by nature.

MICHAEL: I don't want a warm-hearted alien mall rat! I want my son!

ALIEN: How would you have like it if I just walked out right now?

MICHAEL: Better than this!

ALIEN: You don't mean that.

MICHAEL: Oh yes, I do.

(THE ALIEN *stamps out his cigarette.*)

ALIEN: Okay. Have it your way. We'll see how you like it when I'm not around.

MICHAEL: Where are you going?

ALIEN: Out.

MICHAEL: There's no where to go. It's five am. Everything's closed.

ALIEN: That's all right. I can wait. Maybe I'll find somebody who's grateful to have me around.

MICHAEL: But what if I need you? Where are you going?

ALIEN: To find myself a good time! *Ciao*, baby!

(THE ALIEN *takes a swig of coffee, gasps at the punch it packs, and exits.* MICHAEL *stares after him.*)

(Lights out.)

Scene Three

(The same. The next morning. 8:30)

(THE SHERIFF *waits while* MICHAEL *is dressing for work. He listens to the radio playing the triumphant, joyous end of the First Movement of Beethoven's* Seventh Symphony. *It sounds tinny and thin on the radio.)*

(The music pauses for a moment.)

SHERIFF: I just stopped by to....

(The music continues, then finishes.)

SHERIFF: I just stopped by to...

MICHAEL: Shh!

RADIO ANNOUNCER: That was Beethoven's Seventh Symphony, conducted by / / Herbert von Karajan of the Berlin Philharmonic...

MICHAEL: *(Overlapping at //)* What?!

SHERIFF: What's wrong?

MICHAEL: God, I hate it when they do that. I give those guys money.

SHERIFF: What did they do?

MICHAEL: There's another three movements for cryin' out loud! *(To the radio)* Play the whole damn symphony or don't play it at all! *(He flicks off the radio.)* And you could knock.

SHERIFF: *(Forced cheerfulness)* 'morning.

(MICHAEL *starts to put on his K-Mart uniform.)*

(THE SHERIFF *notices the Kierkegaard on the table. He fingers it.)*

SHERIFF: *Fear and Trembling.* Soren...

MICHAEL: Kierkegaard.

SHERIFF: Any good?

MICHAEL: It's a page turner. What time is it?

SHERIFF: Time for some of that good coffee you make.

MICHAEL: It's all gone. Can I please have the time?

SHERIFF: What's the matter, lose your watch?

MICHAEL: I threw out my watch—it only reminded I'm always late.

SHERIFF: It's 8:28.

MICHAEL: I'm late.

SHERIFF: Well, Priscilla called about some sort of problem with Billy.

MICHAEL: Yeah, there's a problem. He's in a spaceship at the moment. As soon as he's back on earth, I'll send him right over. I promise.

SHERIFF: Now, Michael—Billy is her child too. This is no way to deal with...whatever.

MICHAEL: Why can't you just try to believe me, Hank?

SHERIFF: We'd just like to know where Billy is.

MICHAEL: I told you where he is.

SHERIFF: In a spaceship.

MICHAEL: Yes.

SHERIFF: Is there a phone in this spaceship? So maybe we could talk to Billy?

MICHAEL: You know, I'm just guessing—but I bet there isn't.

SHERIFF: Well, a radio then. Some sort of communication device. *(He flips his hand open a la Star Trek)* You know—"Kirk to Enterprise." That kind of thing. So we make sure Billy's okay. It'd take a load off Priscilla's mind, I can tell you.

MICHAEL: If there was some way to talk to Billy, don't you think I would have done it?

SHERIFF: So you haven't talked to him.

MICHAEL: No!

SHERIFF: And you're not planning on it in the near future.

MICHAEL: If I could I would, and I can't!

SHERIFF: All right, okay. Just a thought.

MICHAEL: Look, do you mind? You don't keep K-Mart waiting if you know what's good for you.

SHERIFF: Well, I've got a couple more questions.

(MICHAEL gestures impatiently for him to continue.)

SHERIFF: Priscilla said you mentioned someone else.

MICHAEL: He's not here.

SHERIFF: So there was another person with you.

MICHAEL: It's one of them. An alien.

SHERIFF: I see.

MICHAEL: On the ship he's actually just a busboy.

SHERIFF: What's he doing down here?

MICHAEL: Taking some unauthorized shore leave. He's AWOL.

SHERIFF: An AWOL alien busboy. I never heard of that.

MICHAEL: Well, he's not your science fiction alien. He's a real alien and he has a real life. Not an interesting one necessarily, but a life.

SHERIFF: Where is he now?

MICHAEL: *(Beat)* I don't know.

SHERIFF: No idea?

MICHAEL: No.

SHERIFF: He just left, just like that? Not a word?

MICHAEL: That's right.

SHERIFF: Any guesses which way he was heading?

MICHAEL: Look, they're an advanced race, okay? I don't pretend to know what one of them might be thinking. They're very subtle, very brilliant.

SHERIFF: I thought he was a busboy.

MICHAEL: Well, I'm talking about potential.

SHERIFF: And I'm talking about where he went. Does he drive a car?

MICHAEL: I doubt it.

SHERIFF: So he's hitchhiking.

MICHAEL: Maybe, but I don't think anybody's going to pick him up.

SHERIFF: Why not?

MICHAEL: He has green skin.

SHERIFF: *(Gets an odd look on his face)* Trinkle.

MICHAEL: Excuse me?

SHERIFF: Mrs Trinkle. High school.

MICHAEL: Yeah...?

SHERIFF: You said green skin, and Mrs Trinkle just popped into my head. How do you like that? We did yearbook with her.

MICHAEL: Right. And Senior English.

SHERIFF: Good times. Good years. Huh. Now why the heck do you suppose that came back to me right then?

MICHAEL: Little Proustian moment I guess.

SHERIFF: Yeah, I guess so...a what?

MICHAEL: Never mind, nothing.

SHERIFF: Seems like a long time, doesn't it.

MICHAEL: It is a long time.

SHERIFF: Be nice to go back, though, wouldn't it.

MICHAEL: No, not really.

SHERIFF: We always thought a lot of you, Michael. Always thought you were the one going somewhere. That you were going to get out into the big world.

MICHAEL: Well, I didn't.

SHERIFF: No. You're still here, working at the K-Mart.

MICHAEL: You don't lose your provincialism by leaving the provinces, Hank. This is my big world, right here. (Referring to the book) At least, it's the place I go looking for the big world. I'm not sure I've found it yet.

SHERIFF: Don't you think you'd be better off leaving, though? Going off to Chicago, Minneapolis, New York? Someplace where people could... appreciate you?

MICHAEL: What makes you think they would? Wherever you go, they're still people, aren't they.

SHERIFF: You're frustrated Michael, and you're angry. You want people to understand you, but they don't, and they never will. Not around here.

MICHAEL: So what's this? Is the sheriff telling me to "get out of town"?

SHERIFF: Actually, the sheriff is saying stay put until this whole thing is over. Then get out of town. Find another town—a town where you can be happy, where you fit in. For yourself, I'm talking.

MICHAEL: Sure, no problem. Just one thing.

SHERIFF: What's that?

MICHAEL: Show me the town.

(Lights fade on them.)

Scene Four

(A roadside bar. Lots of different beer signs and a jukebox that doesn't work quite right.)

(RAY is behind the bar. THE ALIEN sits on a barstool, a glass of tap beer in one hand. Something about the lighting of the bar makes his skin look like it's a normal color.)

(10:30 A M)

(THE ALIEN is peering intently at the jukebox. He takes a swig of the tap. When he speaks, it's increasingly rapid fire, as if he's wired on caffeine.)

ALIEN: Hey, what is that thing? That is really cool looking.

RAY: What—you never seen a jukebox before?

(THE ALIEN turns back to it in wonder.)

ALIEN: Oh, a jukebox, a jukebox. Oh man! A jukebox! I heard of those, it's a jukebox. This is incredible.

RAY: 'Course, that one there has the karaoke feature.

ALIEN: No, you're kidding, oh my God, karaoke. *(He polishes off the tap and goes for a closer look.)*

RAY: Oh yeah, we keep up with all the big city trends.

ALIEN: I didn't know if there really was such a thing as karaoke, I mean you hear about karaoke but you're not really sure if something like it really exists because people make things up, you know? They make up all kinds of great things and then you get to a place and it isn't really there and then you're really disappointed and then you get depressed and then you want to sing karaoke even more than you did before, know what I mean?

(RAY is already reaching to open another beer for THE ALIEN.)

RAY: How's about one more?

ALIEN: I don't know—I'm pretty wired.

RAY: What the hey, gonna be noon before you know it. And you look like you need a little somethin' to take the edge off. *(Confidentially, as he hands THE ALIEN the beer.)* I'd have one with you but it's against policy.

ALIEN: I thought you owned the place.

RAY: Well, yeah, I do. But the wife is management. Final word is mine but management pretty much runs the show. She says when I drink behind the bar, the books don't balance at the end of the day.

ALIEN: And neither do you, I bet.

RAY: Eh?

ALIEN: Balance at the end of the day.

RAY: Oh dang. That's a good one. I got to tell the wife that. You're quick on the come backs, ain't you. You and she'd get along great. She's quick on the come backs too.

(THE ALIEN *takes a deep swig as...the sound of a car pulling into the lot outside.* RAY *goes to the window.)*

RAY: That'd be Hank. He's the Sheriff.

ALIEN: Sheriff?

RAY: He come by to talk to the wife. She and her ex are goin' through some trouble on account of he says their boy was abducted by Martians.

ALIEN: Abducted by *Martians...*

RAY: Yeah. How 'bout something original for cryin' outside. *(He looks through the window. He waves and talks—doesn't yell—through the window even though* THE SHERIFF *obviously can't hear him.)* Yup, goin' right around to the back door. Hey Hank. How ya doin'?

(Meanwhile, THE ALIEN *is visibly putting this all together in his head.)*

ALIEN: How's she taking it?

RAY: Priscilla? Not so good. He done this before, of course, but he never said it was Martians. I'd say that was the part got her wound up.

ALIEN: Boy do I feel terrible.

RAY: How come?

ALIEN: Warmhearted by nature.

RAY: Oh.

ALIEN: I just wish there was something I could do.

RAY: When Priscilla's like this, she's in her own world. There's no point in worryin' 'cause there's nothing you're gonna do about it. My advice is you do what I do—drop your dollar in there and sing your heart out.

ALIEN: No, I couldn't. I'm not much of a singer.

RAY: That's what they all say. You'll get the hang of it.

ALIEN: You first. You show me how.

RAY: Well I would but the problem is you don't get professional sound quality when the pipes are dry.

ALIEN: You're a professional singer?

RAY: Well, not exactly. But people're always asking me to get up and knock out an old ballad or two.

ALIEN: Is that right!

RAY: Well, I don't claim to be Mel Torme. But I can hold my own in these parts.

ALIEN: Oh, you have to sing for me! Please!

RAY: No, no. Wife wouldn't like it. Says the karaoke's for customers only.

ALIEN: I'll tell her I made you do it.

RAY: No, serious now. No can do 'less I get a couple in me—

ALIEN: Go on then—they're on me. *(He hands across a hundred dollar bill.)*

RAY: Dang.

ALIEN: And keep the change.

RAY: Well...maybe just one to get the vocal cords warmed up. How's she gonna know, eh?

ALIEN: Dang if I know!

RAY: Now you're talkin'. *(He pops open a beer and takes hit.)* First one of the morning sure tastes sweet, don't it?

ALIEN: Party...down!

(Lights blackout.)

Scene Five

(The office in back of the same bar. Time is continuous from the previous scene. THE SHERIFF stands in the doorway, while PRISCILLA confronts him.)

PRISCILLA: Do you know what Michael said to me two months ago? He had Billy for the afternoon and Billy threw a fit because Michael had thrown out his T V and he couldn't watch *The New Adventures of Hercules.* So Michael comes back to me and says if I keep letting him watch garbage like that, he's going to take matters into his own hands. His words: 'take matters into his own hands.'

SHERIFF: I think about throwing out my T V sometimes.

PRISCILLA: Excuse me, but you're missing the point.

SHERIFF: I think you're missing Michael's point.

PRISCILLA: I want to know what are you going to do about this.

SHERIFF: Well, I searched the woods, the clearing, the quarry. There's no sign of Billy out there.

PRISCILLA: Of course not. Michael wouldn't leave him in the woods. But I'll tell you what he might have done.

SHERIFF: What's that?

PRISCILLA: Drove Billy down to Sheboygan and left him with his Aunt Rho.

SHERIFF: Then why don't you go down there and get him?

PRISCILLA: Because I'm not playing this game with Michael again. He did this same thing last year. It took me three days to figure it out and I finally ended up on a two hour car trip to Sheboygan, listening to him lecture me about my parenting skills and my bad taste in T V shows. So this time, I'm putting it in the hands of the authorities.
    That's you, by the way.

SHERIFF: I'm happy to go pay Aunt Rho a visit.

PRISCILLA: And if he's not there, I want you to arrest Michael.

SHERIFF: Priscilla, I think we could give that a day or two.

PRISCILLA: This is why I stuffed envelopes for your campaign? So you could tell me to wait a day or two?

SHERIFF: If we give him some time, he might just come around on his own.

PRISCILLA: I've got news for you, mister. Sheriffs get voted in and Sheriffs also get voted out. And I've got dirt on you, don't forget that. *(She collects her checkbook, purse, etc. and prepares to go out.)*

SHERIFF: There's no dirt on me.

PRISCILLA: You drive that county car when you go fishing up to Wabeno.

(THE SHERIFF reacts.)

PRISCILLA: Didn't think I knew that, did you. That's against regulations. I could use that in a campaign.

SHERIFF: What point are we trying to make here, exactly?

PRISCILLA: I have a son who is missing.

SHERIFF: You just said he's in Sheboygan with his Aunt Rho.

(She is ready to go.)

PRISCILLA: I said *maybe*. Now, by the time I get back from the wholesaler, I want movement on this. However you do it, that's up to you.

SHERIFF: Priscilla...

PRISCILLA: At least bring him into your office.

SHERIFF: And do what?

PRISCILLA: Put the pressure on, for cryin' out loud!

SHERIFF: I already did that. I stopped by this morning for coffee and I...

PRISCILLA: Hank, now listen. You set a mean speed trap, nobody can touch you on kittens in trees. But the Spanish Inquisition you are not. Can't you see that you've got to—

(RAY *enters.*)

RAY: Priscilla, we got any Blackberry Flavored Brandy in the storeroom?

PRISCILLA: You're interrupting, Ray.

RAY: Well, we got some out-of-towner wants to try Blackberry Flavored Brandy once.

PRISCILLA: You've been drinking, haven't you.

RAY: I ain't been drinking.

PRISCILLA: I smell it on your breath, you weasel.

RAY: I ain't been drinking.

PRISCILLA: If you start drinking up our profits again, I'll take your shotgun off the wall and kill you. Do you understand me?

RAY: *(To* THE SHERIFF*)* I hope you heard that, Hank. That's evidence.

PRISCILLA: Correction...I will divorce you, strip you of all your worldly possessions right down to your jockey briefs, wait until January, and then throw your fat-assed sorry-looking self into the snowbank. Then I will take your shotgun and kill you. Are we clear?

RAY: And if I was fishin' right now, we wouldn't be havin' this conversation! Now best you remember who's the boss around here!

(PRISCILLA *makes a move at* RAY, *who flinches. To* THE SHERIFF...)

RAY: I hope you saw that! *(He makes a fast exit.)*

SHERIFF: It's good to see you two are lettin' your feelings out there.

PRISCILLA: Don't worry your pretty little head about my feelings.

SHERIFF: Well sometimes I do.

PRISCILLA: You had your chance, big boy. It's a little late for regret.

SHERIFF: Priscilla, I'm not talking about that.

PRISCILLA: You'd better not be!

SHERIFF: That was a very long time ago, Priscilla. It was Junior Prom.

PRISCILLA: It was Homecoming.

SHERIFF: Well, I was sorry about it then and I'm sorry now.

PRISCILLA: Me too. If you hadn't dumped me, I could be married to you right now. Instead I married Michael on the rebound. And then I married Ray on the rebound from that. If this keeps up, I'm gonna marry my dog.

SHERIFF: I never dumped you.

PRISCILLA: You most certainly did.

SHERIFF: You're the one who broke it off.

PRISCILLA: Because I would not be humiliated by watching you ask Amy VanderHooven to Homecoming.

SHERIFF: You weren't even speaking to me.

PRISCILLA: Not after you asked Amy VanderHooven!

SHERIFF: Priscilla, this is ancient history. My own son Ethan is set to play in the Homecoming game this year and Amy VanderHooven went lesbian ten years ago. Now come on. We're here, you and me, right now.

PRISCILLA: You're right. Good. Current events then. Right now, Hank, you're the Sheriff. So arrest somebody. *(She exits before he can say anything.)*

(The lights change.)

Scene Six

(The bar. Some time has passed. THE ALIEN *still sits on his bar stool.* RAY *is considerably drunker than before.* RAY *and* THE ALIEN *sing karaoke.)*

RAY: *Volare, oh, oh!*

ALIEN: *Cantare, oh, oh, oh, oh!*
Nel blu, dipinto di blu
Felice di stare lassù grave...

RAY: We can sing in the glow of a star that I know of Where lovers enjoy peace of mind

RAY & ALIEN: *Volare, oh, oh!*
Cantare, oh, oh, oh, oh!

(The song ends.)

ALIEN: *Bravo! Eccellente!*

RAY: *(Modestly)* You're not so bad yourself there once.

ALIEN: *Dovresti cantare per tutta la vita!*

RAY: Not to mention you speak darn good Spanish.

ALIEN: *Grazie.*

RAY: Come to think of it, y'kinda have that olive compleshion. Ya got some Messcan in ya?

ALIEN: God I love this planet—place! I knew I was going to like it, but I had no idea! It's so...well, *earthy. So...honest.*

RAY: That's me.

ALIEN: Do you mind if I ask you something?

RAY: Yeah, sure. I got to siddown though... *(He discovers he's already sitting.)* Okay, shoot.

ALIEN: Suppose some friends of yours did something...upsetting.

RAY: All my frien's are out fishin'.

ALIEN: How about your wife?

RAY: She hates fishin'.

ALIEN: Well, how about the Sheriff?

RAY: Hank likes fishin'.

ALIEN: Okay. Suppose Hank—I don't know—kidnapped somebody.

RAY: He can't do tha', he's th' Sheriff.

ALIEN: It's hypothetical.

RAY: Oh! Awright. I'm with ya.

ALIEN: And you helped him.

RAY: Yeah, tha's *good.*

ALIEN: Not directly, but you provided certain services. But things got a little complicated and people got really wound up about it. In other words you feel just a little bit guilty.

RAY: Guilty!? Hah! I know all about guilty.

ALIEN: Expand.

RAY: Guilty is you promise your best darn fishin' buddies in the whole world that you're gonna spend a couple days at the Flowage, and then you gotta chuck the whole deal at the last second because you're too darn *accommodatin'* to the ball and chain! You're lookin' at somebody with some *issues* here, so don't tell me.

ALIEN: So there's nothing to be done.

RAY: I never said that.

ALIEN: Well what the hey. I'm relyin' on you for the local custom.

RAY: *(With great seriousness)* Canned goods.

ALIEN: Excuse me?

RAY: Nice package of canned goods usually puts it right. *(He places a six pack of bottled beer on the bar.)* Bottles're good too.

ALIEN: What if the situation is touchier than that.

RAY: I'd just go in there, put my arms around 'em, and jes' give 'em a big hug.

ALIEN: What you're saying is, provide comfort.

RAY: Yah.

ALIEN: You know what? You've got a beautiful soul.

RAY: *(Singing)* When the moon hits your eye...

ALIEN: *(Singing)* Like a big pizza pie...

RAY & ALIEN: That's amore!

(Lights change)

Scene Seven

(K-Mart, MICHAEL's place of work. MICHAEL is stacking toy flying saucers onto the shelf. THE SHERIFF hands him boxes.)

MICHAEL: So Billy shows up for the weekend, and flips out because I threw out the T V and he can't watch that Hercules crap—which apparently Ray told him was just like reading classical literature.
Inside, part of me dies. The other part is going to dismember Ray.

SHERIFF: All the kids watch that stuff, Michael.

MICHAEL: This is my son—my flesh and blood, a boy who walked to the C D player when he was five years old and put on Beethoven's *Seventh Symphony* all by himself.

SHERIFF: Well at least it wasn't *Xena: Warrior Princess*. That one's got too much sex and violence.

MICHAEL: Hank, you're missing the point.

SHERIFF: Well I think you're missing Priscilla's point.

MICHAEL: That *Hercules* show takes a timeless myth that penetrates to the core of our collective psyche, rips out every shred of meaning, and gives us back the empty shell. The myth of Hercules is about guilt and courage and innocence and rage—and sex and violence for that matter, but real sex and real violence. With real causes and real consequences. That T V show is about a guy with big muscles and long hair!

SHERIFF: Well sex and violence wasn't the same thing in the old days.

MICHAEL: What are you talking about?

SHERIFF: They weren't so down and dirty back then.

MICHAEL: Are you kidding?! What about *Anna Karenina*?

SHERIFF: If that's on cable, we don't get that...

MICHAEL: *Anna Karenina*. It's a book. It was an assignment senior year!

SHERIFF: Well I never got to it!

MICHAEL: *Hamlet* then! We had that too! *A Streetcar Named Desire*! *Crime and Punishment*!

SHERIFF: Okay I get the...

MICHAEL: *The Iliad*! *The Odyssey*! *The Bible*!

SHERIFF: Michael, okay.

MICHAEL: Sex and violence galore!

SHERIFF: Okay, I got it.

MICHAEL: You don't got it.

SHERIFF: I'm not a total rock head, Michael. I got it!

MICHAEL: Priscilla was never like this when she was with me! It's Ray's fault.

SHERIFF: Priscilla is happy in her new life, Michael. One of these days you have to accept that.

MICHAEL: She is not happy with him.

SHERIFF: Priscilla's as happy as Priscilla gets. She's not an easy woman to please.

MICHAEL: I pleased her.

SHERIFF: Well, apparently—no.

MICHAEL: I was good for her.

SHERIFF: She divorced you.

MICHAEL: Ultimately, yes, but in the meantime we had some good years.

SHERIFF: No you didn't.

MICHAEL: Well—months, anyway.

SHERIFF: Everything always comes back to Priscilla in your mind. You're fixated on her. You've got to let go of that anger.

Now look, I want to clear up a couple things before I head to Sheboygan. Did you threaten to take Billy if he, uh... *(He consults a notebook.)* ...if his home environment didn't get better?

MICHAEL: Did she tell you that?

SHERIFF: Yes or no?

MICHAEL: I was just spouting off about Ray. She knows that.

SHERIFF: What's so bad about Ray? He's a solid guy.

MICHAEL: He's a moron.

SHERIFF: He's a typical, regular guy.

MICHAEL: Exactly.

SHERIFF: All right, now look. I got to ask you to come down to the station for a few minutes.

MICHAEL: The station?

SHERIFF: I am conducting an investigation. It's standard procedure.

MICHAEL: You've been waiting for this for twenty years, haven't you! Ever since I quit the bowling team to take oboe lessons.

SHERIFF: Will you please come down with me?

MICHAEL: No.

SHERIFF: Michael, I'm asking you nicely.

MICHAEL: Well, are you asking me or telling me?

SHERIFF: I'm asking you.

MICHAEL: I'm not going down to the station with any guy who's never read *Anna Karenina*.

SHERIFF: Michael, I don't want to arrest you.

MICHAEL: Why not?

SHERIFF: I don't want to do the paper work.

MICHAEL: Then I'm not going.

SHERIFF: *(Beat)* All right, all right. I'll meet you half way. How's that?

MICHAEL: How's what?

SHERIFF: You come down to the station by your own choice—no fuss, and I'll read that, uh, Anna Kara-what's-her-name for you.

MICHAEL: You're kidding me, right?

SHERIFF: I'm dead serious. No guarantee I'm going to understand it, mind you. But I'll crack the old binding there. Or if you insist, we'll do it the old fashioned way. It's up to you.

MICHAEL: Hank, this whole thing is unfair. It's embarrassing and it's downright unfriendly. But the thought of you reading *Anna Karenina* almost makes it worthwhile.

SHERIFF: So is it a deal?

(MICHAEL *gestures for him to lead the way.*)

MICHAEL: Take me to your leader.

(MICHAEL *exits, followed by* THE SHERIFF.)

(*The lights cross fade.*)

Scene Eight

(*The bar.* RAY *is asleep—passed out—on the top of the bar. He snores.* THE ALIEN *finishes off his beer and walks around to the back of the bar. He pours himself a big cup of coffee.*)

(*He's about to drink it when* PRISCILLA *appears behind him, coming in from the back with a carton of bottles.*)

PRISCILLA: And just what do you think you're doing?

ALIEN: Oh. I paid for this.

PRISCILLA: What am I, stupid? Get out from behind there.

ALIEN: You can ask, Ray. I paid in advance. I'm covered.

PRISCILLA: Mister, don't mess with me. The Sheriff's a friend of mine and I've got a twelve gauge right back there. Now move it on out.

ALIEN: Under protest.

PRISCILLA: Under anything you want, just do it.

(*He comes out from behind the bar. She goes behind it herself.*)

ALIEN: You must be Priscilla.

(RAY *snorts.*)

ALIEN: Ray here speaks highly of you.

PRISCILLA: Ray here drinks in the middle of the day.

ALIEN: So do I.

PRISCILLA: Some people can hold it.

ALIEN: It did seem to knock him up.

PRISCILLA: Out.

ALIEN: What?

PRISCILLA: Knock him out.

ALIEN: Right. Knock him *out.*

PRISCILLA: Any excuse to take a nap or go limp. That's my Ray.

(RAY snorts.)

ALIEN: I need to say two things. First, this is my fault and I'm sorry. Don't be angry with him. If you must be angry with someone, I'm the one.

PRISCILLA: What's the other thing?

ALIEN: You're unhappy.

PRISCILLA: Yeah, well—you would be too, believe me.

ALIEN: Yes, Ray told me about Billy. But that's not what I meant. I meant something deeper. Something very basic.

PRISCILLA: My emotional condition is none of your concern.

ALIEN: But it is my concern. No man is an island, entire of itself; every man is a piece of the continent, a part of the main; if a clod be washed away by the sea, Europe is the less, as well as if a promontory were, as well as if a manor of thy friend's or of thy own were; any man's death diminishes me, because I am involved in mankind; and therefore never send to know for whom the bell tolls; it tolls for thee.

PRISCILLA: *(Fascinated, softening in spite of herself)* Not local, are you.

ALIEN: No, but I like the neighborhood.

PRISCILLA: You ought to be meet my ex-husband. You and he'd get along great.

ALIEN: I'm not so sure about that. I bet he prefers women.

(She laughs out loud.)

PRISCILLA: Last time I checked.

(Pause. They look at each other. She's unsure of herself but liking it.)

ALIEN: I thought you were leaving.

ALIEN: We were discussing your melancholy state of mind.

PRISCILLA: Nice of you to care—but what makes you so interested?

ALIEN: I told you. I am involved in mankind.

PRISCILLA: Oh yeah. I'm impressed by the way. You know that whole speech. How did that happen?

ALIEN: No, let's talk about you instead.

PRISCILLA: Uh-unh.

ALIEN: I memorized it.

PRISCILLA: Why?

ALIEN: Your turn. Tell me your sorrows.

PRISCILLA: No. Why did you memorize it?

ALIEN: Because I had to. They made me.

PRISCILLA: They?

ALIEN: My...employers. It was part of a training program. They made us learn all kinds of information about your, our world. You know—culture, science, mating rituals. I couldn't care less about it, to tell you the truth. Except for that one part. "I am involved." That part I get.

(Beat)

PRISCILLA: Life stinks.

ALIEN: Expand.

PRISCILLA: You divorce your husband number one and he kidnaps your little boy. And the Sheriff who dumped you just before Homecoming, and who you helped get elected to office, won't lift a finger to get him back. Then there's hubbie number two, who you married because he impressed you by being outdoorsy and fun-loving and he looked great on a Harley— only now you can't even leave him in charge of the family business for two hours but you come back to find him in his usual state of arousal.

(She indicates RAY, passed out. He snorts.)

ALIEN: But a hundred dollars richer.

(She looks and finds the money.)

ALIEN: Told you—I paid in advance.

PRISCILLA: What do you do? Print it yourself?

ALIEN: No, other people do that for me.

PRISCILLA: Oh, rich kid, huh?

ALIEN: Rich enough to take you away from all this.

PRISCILLA: Yeah? Where would we go?

ALIEN: How about to the moon and back?

PRISCILLA: I want to go wherever my kid is.

ALIEN: Oh.

PRISCILLA: Can't manage that one, can you.

ALIEN: No. Not really.

PRISCILLA: Didn't think so.

ALIEN: But I'm sure he'll be back.

PRISCILLA: You're very nice but your being sure is just not good enough.

ALIEN: I promise you, he'll come back. All safe and sound.

PRISCILLA: Listen, what do you know? Huh? You don't have a crazy ex-husband and you probably don't have kids either, do you. So what would you know? Huh? What would you know about these feelings? You don't know anything.

ALIEN: I'm sorry you're upset.

PRISCILLA: One thing I don't need is sympathy!

ALIEN: Yes it is.

PRISCILLA: No it is not!

ALIEN: Everybody needs sympathy.

PRISCILLA: I am not everybody. I am Priscilla Zuelke. *(Pronounced ZULL-key. Rhymes with FULL-key)* I do not need anything, anytime, from anyone.

ALIEN: Then what do you want?

PRISCILLA: Someone who'll listen to me when I talk.

ALIEN: It must be awful, not having anyone to listen.

PRISCILLA: It is awful!

ALIEN: Of course it is.

PRISCILLA: You don't know. It's always me who has to listen and I can't do it anymore! It's...it's...it's...!

(She breaks down and cries.)

ALIEN: Go ahead. Have a good cry.

(She cries. He strokes her shoulder.)

ALIEN: That's right. Let it out. Let it out.

PRISCILLA: Oh God! It's...too much!

ALIEN: Yes, it is.

PRISCILLA: It's too much for one person!

ALIEN: It is, you're right. It isn't fair. *(He moves in closer and embraces her lightly.)* You've been very brave.

PRISCILLA: No I haven't.

ALIEN: Yes, you've kept a very level head through all of this.

PRISCILLA: How would you know?

ALIEN: I've got eyes. I see how you are. You're strong. But when it's too much, it's too much. A person can only take so much.

PRISCILLA: That's right. *(She stops crying.)* You're touching me.

ALIEN: Is it all right?

PRISCILLA: Well, no, not really.

ALIEN: Why not?

PRISCILLA: Because my husband is right there.

ALIEN: He's asleep.

PRISCILLA: People wake up.

ALIEN: Eventually.

PRISCILLA: No really. I...I didn't want this.

ALIEN: I know. But I can't help it. I listened.

PRISCILLA: But Ray...

ALIEN: I can't help you there. But I can help you here.

PRISCILLA: Oh

ALIEN: If you want me to.

PRISCILLA: I...I don't know...

ALIEN: I think you do know.

PRISCILLA: I think I do too. *(She kisses him, then pulls away.)* Not here.

ALIEN: Yes.

PRISCILLA: No, there's an apartment upstairs.

ALIEN: I don't like apartments.

PRISCILLA: But...

ALIEN: He won't wake up for hours.

PRISCILLA: How do you know?

ALIEN: I know. I know more than you think.

(He presses her against the bar, kisses her passionately, and they begin to make love.)

(Lights fade.)

Scene Nine

(The same, evening. MICHAEL is at the front door. He sees RAY asleep on the bar.)

MICHAEL: Hey. Wake up. Wake up. Ray, wake up.

RAY: Oh gawd...

MICHAEL: Come on. Wake up.

RAY: Pr'cilla's not here.

MICHAEL: I'm not looking for Priscilla.

RAY: Well, sh'snot here.

MICHAEL: Will you please wake up?

RAY: I'm'wake.

(But his eyes stay shut. MICHAEL walks around the bar, pours a glass of water and throws it in RAY's face. RAY opens his eyes.)

RAY: Thank you.

MICHAEL: I thought you stopped drinking during the day.

RAY: This was social. I was pressured.

MICHAEL: By whom?

RAY: Some drunk, that's whom. Who else stands outside a bar at 10 o'clock in the morning?

MICHAEL: How did he look?

RAY: He looked like a drunk with a bad case of liver damage. Worst looking skin I ever saw.

MICHAEL: Sort of...green?

RAY: I'd say more like yellow. Inside the bar here, he didn't look so bad—neon lights, you know. But outside in the daylight...whoo-ee. Scary. Hell of a nice guy, though. *(He goes behind the bar and pours himself a little hair of the dog.)*

MICHAEL: Where did he go?

RAY: I don't know.

MICHAEL: When did he leave?

RAY: I don't know.

MICHAEL: You mean, you passed out while he was still here?

RAY: When you pass out, you don't have much say over when.

MICHAEL: Did he say where he was going?

RAY: He just said he had to take off.

MICHAEL: Take off?

RAY: Yeah, get goin'.

MICHAEL: Well, did he say "get going," or did he say "take off"?

RAY: What difference does it make? He left, okay?

MICHAEL: It makes a lot of difference!

RAY: Well I can't remember.

MICHAEL: Well, the first time you said 'take off.'

RAY: Okay.

MICHAEL: So is that it? Is that what he said?

RAY: Yeah. Okay? That's what he said.

MICHAEL: You don't even know, do you?

RAY: No, I don't know! The rest of us aren't so perfect, Mike. I never went to college, I don't take notes!

MICHAEL: That's not what this is about!

RAY: Oh really? Then what's it about?

MICHAEL: That drunk was an alien! He's one of them, you dolt! He was at my house this morning. I got angry and like an idiot I let him walk out on me, and now I have absolutely no idea where he is and he's my only contact with Billy, so it's somewhat crucial that I find him!

(Slight pause)

RAY: Holy moley—you're really all holes and no cheese, ain't ya?

MICHAEL: Didn't it occur to you even once? You sat there and listened to me last night talking about the aliens and how they took Billy, and this morning a green-skinned man shows up at your bar?

RAY: I didn't say green, I said yellow. Liver damage don't make you green.

MICHAEL: But maybe this wasn't liver damage, Ray.

RAY: Hey, gimme some credit one time. I know something on the subject, okay? This guy was yellow.

MICHAEL: That's because you see the world through the light of an Old Milwaukee sign!

RAY: I took your wife, Mike. Okay? I'm sorry about that. But there's no need to get personal.

MICHAEL: You did not take Priscilla.

RAY: Well, she's married to me, whether anybody likes it or not.

MICHAEL: Priscilla left me, Ray. You had nothing to do with it! *(He starts to leave.)*

RAY: You never loved her.

(MICHAEL stops.)

MICHAEL: I loved her.

RAY: Well you sure as heck never understood her.

MICHAEL: I understood her. Better than you ever will. There's a song inside her and someday she's going to sing it and believe me, the tune will not be Ray Zuelke.

(MICHAEL exits. RAY calls after him.)

RAY: Well boo-hoo! You're really breakin' my heart! And what's more, Priscilla's tone-deaf!

(We hear PRISCILLA's lovely voice from the back, singing. RAY meanwhile gets a cold cloth from behind the bar. He sits down in a chair and presses the cloth across his eyes as PRISCILLA enters.)

PRISCILLA: "Blue moon
You saw me standing alone
Without a dream in my heart
Without a—
(She sees RAY, who has taken off the cloth and is looking at her.) Oh. Hello.

RAY: I'm sorry, Priscilla.

PRISCILLA: Sit, sit. *(She puts a fresh cloth on him.)* I'll get you fresh.

RAY: Priscilla, if you're winding up for the pitch, go ahead and let fly. I'm ready for it.

PRISCILLA: What pitch? Head back.

RAY: About how I uh—took a little nap at the bar.

PRISCILLA: "Got drunk and passed out" you mean, don't you.

RAY: Yes Priscilla.

PRISCILLA: I know we have our troubles, Ray. And I don't know where it goes from here, but from now on, let's both of us say what we mean and mean what we say.

RAY: Yeah, okay. I know you're angry at me.

PRISCILLA: Ray, I'm not angry.

RAY: You're not?

PRISCILLA: Sometimes the world is a surprising place. Unplanned. Beautiful. And if you let yourself be surprised, if you're unafraid, if you accept that anything is possible but that nothing is certain, then you can really live. We spend most of our lives turning away from that ecstacy, denying it, refusing it. Fearing it. It's too beautiful, it asks too much of us. But when we find it— Angry Ray? I just can't find it in myself.

RAY: Priscilla.

PRISCILLA: Yes, Ray.

RAY: *(Testing)* I'm goin' to meet the boys tomorrow morning up to the Flowage.

PRISCILLA: That sounds lovely.

RAY: The Flowage, Priscilla, real early—and we won't get back 'til late.

PRISCILLA: Have a wonderful time. *Arrivederci! (She kisses him on the forehead.)*

(Lights fade)

Scene Ten

(A clearing in the woods. THE ALIEN *sits, reading an* Us *magazine, and wearing a Walkman.* MICHAEL *enters in a hurry. He stops abruptly when he sees* THE ALIEN*.)*

MICHAEL: I knew it! I've been looking all over for you! You're waiting for them, aren't you. They're coming back.

ALIEN: No comment.

MICHAEL: Why else would you be out here?

ALIEN: Michael, it would be better if you went home.

MICHAEL: I'm staying right where I am. I want to be here when Billy steps off that ship.

*(*THE ALIEN *offers no further resistance.* MICHAEL *sighs, annoyed, and sits down.)*

MICHAEL: I should have brought a jacket. Don't you get cold?

ALIEN: All the time.

MICHAEL: You don't look cold.

ALIEN: You get used to it.

MICHAEL: I guess it's always cold in outer space.

ALIEN: Yeah, and no one can hear you scream either. That movie scared the crap out of me. Checked under my bunk for a month.

MICHAEL: How do you know all these movies, anyway?

ALIEN: The T V signal. It doesn't stop when it gets to your T V set, you know. It keeps going, out into space.

MICHAEL: No. *(Beat)* So I'm not supposed to be here when they bring him back.

ALIEN: Not really, no.

MICHAEL: I was here when they took him, wasn't I?

ALIEN: That was a mistake.

MICHAEL: So they make mistakes.

ALIEN: Are you kidding? Why do you think we keep coming back? Because interstellar travel is such a treat? Because our thirst for knowledge cannot be assuaged? No. Because they can't get it right. That's why.

MICHAEL: What have you got to be so bitter about?

ALIEN: All my life, I was subjected to all the snooty high brow culture you can imagine: Ludwig Van Beethoven—

MICHAEL: They know Beethoven?

ALIEN: They love Beethoven. And Shakespeare and Ibsen. And Marxist theory, Plato and Aristotle, Rembrandt and Titian, Goethe and Dickens and Tolstoy and blah dee blah dee blah!
     But Michael, all I wanted was to listen to The Spice Girls, to flip through the new *Us* Magazine, to watch Friends. That's what I came down here for. Is that such a terrible thing?

MICHAEL: I wouldn't say terrible—but is it worth coming all the way across the galaxy for?

ALIEN: To me, it is. Anyway, I had one good day. I wish there'd be a few more, that's all. *(He stands up suddenly.)* Hold on! Hold on!...

MICHAEL: What's wrong?

ALIEN: I'm getting a message.

MICHAEL: What kind of message?

ALIEN: Shh! *(Beat)* They're not coming. They're turning back.

MICHAEL: What?

ALIEN: Further tests.

MICHAEL: They can't do that.

ALIEN: They just did.

MICHAEL: Oh come on!

ALIEN: I'm sorry! They just sent word.

MICHAEL: Just when sent word? You have a radio?

ALIEN: It's not a radio.

MICHAEL: Well, what is it?

ALIEN: It's this doohickey.

MICHAEL: A doohickey?

ALIEN: A Telepathy Enhancement Device. They send messages and I listen.

MICHAEL: If you're AWOL, how do they know to be sending you messages?

ALIEN: They're not sending me messages. It's an open channel. I get everything.

MICHAEL: Well, I don't see any doohickey.

ALIEN: It's implanted.

MICHAEL: Where?

ALIEN: *(With his finger in his mouth)* Ith in 'ere.

MICHAEL: Look, I want him back. I want my son back! *(He moves closer, grabbing THE ALIEN.)*

ALIEN: You'll get him back! Don't worry about it!

MICHAEL: When?!

ALIEN: Before sunrise!

MICHAEL: Which sunrise?

ALIEN: I don't know!

MICHAEL: Well, ask them!

ALIEN: How can I ask them?!

MICHAEL: Use the doohickey.

ALIEN: It doesn't work that way. You can't talk into it.

MICHAEL: What kind of radio is that, you can't talk into it. *(He threatens THE ALIEN physically again.)*

ALIEN: It's not a radio, and it's one-way! They talk to me, I can't talk to them!

MICHAEL: You're lying to me!

ALIEN: Why would I lie!?

MICHAEL: Because it doesn't make any sense! What if you were in trouble? What if you needed help? What if somebody were going to kill you? Huh?

ALIEN: You wouldn't hurt me. You're bluffing.

MICHAEL: Wouldn't I?

ALIEN: You wouldn't hurt a flea.

MICHAEL: But you're not a flea, you're an alien. What if I were just pissed off enough—what if I wanted my son back just enough that I said I was going to murder you if you didn't get him back here?! What would happen then? Would your little one way doohickey turn into a two way doohickey? Well?! *(Pause)* Well? Would it? *(He has* THE ALIEN *down on the ground now.)*

ALIEN: No!

MICHAEL: I'll kill you.

ALIEN: You wouldn't!

MICHAEL: I will if I have to! I'm not lying!

ALIEN: Yes you are!

MICHAEL: Do they hear you now? Do they hear what you're saying? Do they hear what I'm saying? *(Into the void)* Do you hear what I'm saying?!

ALIEN: No, they can't!

*(*MICHAEL *is still clutching him.)*

ALIEN: Don't you get it, Michael? It's because I don't really matter. If they lose me, life goes on. The mission goes on. I'm extra. I'm the throw away.
    That's who I am. You didn't get some cosmic Einstein, some messiah from another planet. You got me.

*(*MICHAEL *lets go of him and stands. He looks up at the sky.)*

MICHAEL: I'm sorry.

ALIEN: Yeah. Me too.

MICHAEL: He's really not coming.

ALIEN: Not tonight.

(Pause)

MICHAEL: It's cold.

ALIEN: Yup.

MICHAEL: Well, I'm going back.

ALIEN: To sleep?

MICHAEL: If I can.

ALIEN: Sometimes you can't sleep?

MICHAEL: Not if I'm wound up.

ALIEN: Are you wound up?

MICHAEL: You could say that. Listen, why don't you come back to the
house. We could talk.

ALIEN: What is there to talk about?

MICHAEL: You could tell me more about where you're from.

ALIEN: You don't want to know about that.

MICHAEL: How do you know?

ALIEN: It's boring. It's a boring place. They're all a bunch of boring self-
important snobs. They're so self-important it makes me want to puke.

MICHAEL: Then come back and watch T V.

ALIEN: I thought you threw it out.

MICHAEL: I'll buy another one first thing in the morning. It'll be cheap,
I've got employee discount.

ALIEN: You wouldn't mind?

MICHAEL: I could have had you tracked down, you know. You could be in
the slammer right now. And I could have shown this whole town that I'm
not loony tunes. But I didn't. I don't know why exactly—but there you go.
    Come back. I'll make some nice cold coffee. My special blend—French
Roast with a hint of hazelnut.

ALIEN: What about you?

MICHAEL: I've got a very nice single malt I've been saving for the right
occasion.

ALIEN: It's a deal.

MICHAEL: Come on, then. We'll listen to the radio. It's not much, but on
a clear night I can pick up Chicago.

ALIEN: All the way to Chicago...! Impressive.

(MICHAEL *gestures for* THE ALIEN *to go ahead of him.* THE ALIEN *exits.*
MICHAEL *is about to follow when he stops to look up at the sky.*)

(*The lights fade.*)

END OF ACT ONE

ACT TWO

Scene One

(A T V talk show set)

(MICHAEL sits on one chair, PRISCILLA in another. They're a few feet apart.)

(THE ALIEN stands off to one side, with a hand held mike. He has that slightly unctuous tone of a talk show host.)

ALIEN: We're back with Michael and Priscilla, and the question we're trying to deal with today is: what do you do when your ex-husband says he didn't kidnap your little boy—aliens did!

(Over MICHAEL's head a sign appears that reads "Says His Son Was Kidnapped By Aliens.")

ALIEN: But Priscilla his ex-wife, just isn't having any of it!

(Over PRISCILLA's head a sign that reads "Doesn't Believe A Word He Says.")

ALIEN: So, Priscilla—I have a question for you. Did he ever lie to you when you were married to him?

MICHAEL: I never lied to her.

PRISCILLA: This is my question.

MICHAEL: I never lied to her.

PRISCILLA: *(To THE ALIEN)* Would you tell him it's my turn?

ALIEN: Michael, please—you'll get your chance.

PRISCILLA: It wasn't that he lied, exactly.

MICHAEL: I never lied.

PRISCILLA: Let's just say he had certain problems perceiving reality.

MICHAEL: That is not true.

PRISCILLA: When we first got married, he told me that, when he was a little boy, he used to fly down off his roof.

MICHAEL: I never said that.

PRISCILLA: Yes you did Michael.

MICHAEL: I said it was like flying.

PRISCILLA: You always said, "I flew off the roof and went flying around the yard."

MICHAEL: Because that's how it felt. *(To* THE ALIEN*)* I built a home-made glider when I was a kid.

PRISCILLA: Sure, he tells you that. For years, I never heard the home-made glider part. All I ever heard was: "I flew off my roof."

MICHAEL: You used to love that story.

PRISCILLA: I used to love a lot of things about you until I found out you were a pathological liar. *(To* THE ALIEN*)* He used to make stuff up about our little boy too. Used to insist that Billy put on a Beethoven symphony when he was five years old, all by himself. Except Billy thought he was putting on the soundtrack to Beethoven, that St. Bernard movie!

ALIEN: Okay, okay. But we're looking for something really, deeply strange about Michael. Can you dig down, try to really give us something good?

PRISCILLA: *(Slight beat)* He once told me that he saw angels on the ceiling of the church.

MICHAEL: Because I did.

PRISCILLA: You did not.

MICHAEL: Yes I did.

PRISCILLA: No you didn't Michael.

MICHAEL: Yes I did. *(To* THE ALIEN*)* I saw them.

PRISCILLA: *(Throwing up her hands)* Uh!

(THE ALIEN *holds up the microphone to* THE SHERIFF, *who is in the audience.)*

ALIEN: Yes sir.

SHERIFF: *(Holding up* Anna Karenina.*)* Michael, this Anna Karenina is nothing but sex and violence.

ALIEN: *(Going back to* MICHAEL*)* Thank you.

SHERIFF: *(To* MICHAEL*)* And I'm lovin' every word of it! *(To "the camera")* Hello Ethan!

ALIEN: *(Back with* MICHAEL*)* So Michael, you saw actual angels on the ceiling of your church.

MICHAEL: I certainly did.

PRISCILLA: Nobody else saw them. All anybody else saw was the reflections of the sun off the windshields of cars that were passing by outside.

MICHAEL: I saw the same thing—it's just that I saw something more. I saw what those reflections meant!

PRISCILLA: You see? He admits he never saw angels!

MICHAEL: Priscilla, it's a metaphor. *(To* THE ALIEN*)* She pretends she doesn't know things, but she does.

PRISCILLA: And he's condescending!

MICHAEL: Condescending?! Because I give you credit?

*(*THE ALIEN *goes to* RAY, *also in the audience.)*

ALIEN: Yes sir, go ahead.

RAY: I got a question.

ALIEN: Go ahead.

RAY: My question is you don't know dick! Whaddya think of that?!

ALIEN: Thank you so much. *(Back to* MICHAEL*)* Michael, let me get this straight. You saw a metaphorical angel.

PRISCILLA: A normal person would say he made it up!

MICHAEL: That's right. Metaphorical.

ALIEN: But real angels are different than metaphorical ones, wouldn't you say?

MICHAEL: All angels are metaphorical. They are an expression of the deity.

PRISCILLA: You see how he gets? *(To* MICHAEL*)* You're a snob, you know that?

ALIEN: Priscilla, hold on a second...

PRISCILLA: *(To* THE ALIEN*)* That's exactly the way he talks to me all the time.

MICHAEL: Because you sell yourself short!

ALIEN: So you never saw a real angel. And you lied about that.

MICHAEL: I did not lie about it. I saw real angels.

ALIEN: But they were reflections of some kind of light.

MICHAEL: In my mind, they were real. And that's where angels are real— in your mind.

ALIEN: And the aliens, where are they? Where are they, Michael? In the spaceship—or in your mind? Hold that thought, Michael. We're going to take a break. Back after these messages! *(He exits.)*

MICHAEL: Aliens are nothing at all like angels. Aliens are just people who come from other planets. They're perfectly ordinary people.

PRISCILLA: *(To* MICHAEL*)* You got caught. He's smarter than you.

MICHAEL: A lot of people are smarter than I am.

PRISCILLA: You got your tit caught in the ringer, Michael. *(She stands up to leave.)*

MICHAEL: Where are you going? I'm on television! Don't leave me alone out here! Priscilla, you can't leave!

PRISCILLA: Got to run! I've got a little something in the oven.

(She stands up and we see she's pregnant. She exits.)

(MICHAEL pursues her as far as the door. Throughout the next speech, the overhead signs lift out of sight, the lights change.)

(MICHAEL calls after her, frantically—)

MICHAEL: I did fly! What I did was the same thing as flying. You have no grasp of metaphor! A metaphor is not unreal, it's just a different kind of reality. A deeper, truer kind, as a matter of fact, but you need a little imagination to get to it. And that's what's wrong with you and everybody else in this town. Lack of imagination. Fantasy is good, it's healthy, it's normal. And if you knew the first thing about medieval theology, you'd know I was right about angels, too. They are a manifestation of the deity, and so are our thoughts, so don't tell me I'm crazy just because I happen to believe in levels of reality that you can't begin to appreciate.

(He realizes he's no longer on the tv set, but back in his own house. It's night. At the same time, THE ALIEN has entered looking decidedly queasy.)

MICHAEL: What's wrong?

ALIEN: I'm sick....

MICHAEL: What's the matter?

ALIEN: Too many Gummy Bears and not enough fiber. How about you?

MICHAEL: Just...talking to myself—

ALIEN: I thought maybe you were doing your nightly dramatic reading of Ibsen.

MICHAEL: Taking a break, actually. *(He picks up a rather thick book.)* I'm on the last play.

ALIEN: When We Dead Awaken...

MICHAEL: You know it?

ALIEN: Very well, actually. I made them give it to me on C D-ROM because I hate to read, but Ibsen sort of grows on you.

MICHAEL: Are you sure you're not sick?

ALIEN: I went out for some fresh air and it suddenly hit me. What I'm missing up there on the ship, it's not pre-popped popcorn and a stack of Jackie Chan movies. Well, I am missing that actually, but there's something else. Something a little deeper. It took me ten days of total immersion in your civilization to make me realize—I love earth because I love the people. I want human contact.

MICHAEL: What's wrong, I don't qualify?

ALIEN: But you don't need me, Michael. You're just like them. You've got everything you want right here. Ibsen, Kierkegaard, Beethoven—
Michael, I like you. *(Referring to all his pop culture junk...)* And I appreciate how you helped me out. But I'm not anything you want me to be.

MICHAEL: No one is what I want them to be. I'm not what I want me to be. But I could help you. You could learn to appreciate great literature. It's wonderful and exciting—it's—it's—

ALIEN: I know, it's "The eye of our dreams and the pilot of our souls."

MICHAEL: Yes! You do understand! And you just confessed to liking Ibsen....

ALIEN: Well, I—

MICHAEL: Come on try this with me just once. We could divide up the parts.

ALIEN: Michael, no—

MICHAEL: You're obviously a good reader. Why not just try it?

ALIEN: Michael because I just don't care!

(Beat)

MICHAEL: Right. Okay. I won't ever ask again.

ALIEN: Tomorrow morning, I'd like to go out.

MICHAEL: Where to?

ALIEN: Well, that first day—I made a friend.

MICHAEL: What kind of friend?

ALIEN: Just someone I liked.

MICHAEL: A female type friend?

ALIEN: Not that it matters, but yes.

MICHAEL: Nice.

ALIEN: You see, I don't know how much longer I have here, but I want to go find her, spend whatever time I have.

MICHAEL: Does she know you're an alien?

ALIEN: Not exactly. The lighting was dim.

MICHAEL: Well you can't go to her looking like that.

ALIEN: Like what?

MICHAEL: You skin is green.

ALIEN: She won't care about that. She's not that type.

MICHAEL: Look, let me go down to the drugstore in the morning and pick up some makeup. Just enough to give you rosy cheeks. I'll bring it home at lunch.

ALIEN: You don't mind?

MICHAEL: They already think I'm pretty strange downtown. Buying a little Maybelline won't make much difference now.

ALIEN: Thank you, Michael.

MICHAEL: Well...back to Henrik.

ALIEN: "We'll see what we've lost only when we dead awaken."

MICHAEL: You remember it?

ALIEN: It's Irene, isn't it? "We'll see that we've never really lived until now."

MICHAEL: And then high up in the mountains, we hear Maja singing—
"I am free! I am free! I am free!
No more living in cages for me!

MICHAEL & ALIEN: I am free as a bird! I am free!"

(Lights out.)

Scene Two

(K-Mart, later that morning. A Blue Light on the top of a pole. It's not on.)

(MICHAEL is up on a short stepladder. THE SHERIFF is beside the ladder carrying a yearbook and Anna Karenina.*)*

SHERIFF: I'm up to page forty on *Anna K.* by the way. It's not so bad but I'm only clockin' a chapter a day, 'cause I don't want Ethan to catch me with it and get interested. It's a little too racy for him.
   What are you doing?

MICHAEL: I'm going to electrocute myself.

I'm kidding. It's a broken blue light, Hank. K-Mart without an operational blue light is not K-Mart as we know it.

(THE SHERIFF holds the ladder.)

SHERIFF: I got to thinking about our little talk when I remembered Mrs Trinkle? What'd you call that moment?

MICHAEL: Proustian.

SHERIFF: Right. Something about that kept nagging at me. So I got out my old annuals. And I looked through them. And right there, in our junior year, we did a play. A Mrs Trinkle original—"M Is for Martian". You were in it. You remember what you played?

MICHAEL: ...yes.

SHERIFF: What did you play?

MICHAEL: Hank, this is not relevant.

SHERIFF: What did you play, Michael?

MICHAEL: The Martian.

SHERIFF: And what color skin did you have in the play?

MICHAEL: Green.

SHERIFF: That's right. Color picture right here in the annual.

MICHAEL: Well Sherlock, you've done it again. Time to break out the cocaine and play the violin.

SHERIFF: Michael, please, I am asking you one last time. What did you do with Billy!?

MICHAEL: I didn't do anything.

SHERIFF: Michael...

MICHAEL: Sometimes, Hank, things just happen. Things are imposed. Things we don't want. This is one of those things, Hank. I did not want Billy taken, she did not want Billy taken, you did not want Billy taken. But Billy was taken. It's none of our doing. And there's nothing we can do about it. This is not about psychology or human will. It's the quintessential existentialist crisis, Hank: what do you do when you can do nothing? You fix the Blue Light. So that even if the world frustrates you, even if you have no place to go, and no one to go to if you did—even then, at least there will still be a Blue Light Special. At least that.

SHERIFF: That's real good. Real nice.
    But I got some news of my own. This has been draggin' on for too long now and I've got a responsibility to the public to wrap things up. If Billy's not back by nine o'clock tonight, I'm going to have to lock you up.

MICHAEL: Of course you are.

SHERIFF: It'll be out of my hands then, Michael. That could mean no more visitation rights. You could even land in prison.

MICHAEL: Then why not arrest me right now? This isn't very good police work.

SHERIFF: It's lousy dang police work! It's called friendship! No matter what I do, I can't make you see that.

You've got this way of seeing the world that's so much more complicated and interesting and weird than anything I could ever dream up, but you can't see something as simple as that.

Now look, wherever you've got him, just bring Billy back. Then get out of here and go someplace where people might see the world the way you do.

Darn it, Michael, do yourself the favor. Or if that's not good enough, then do it for me. For friendship.

MICHAEL: *(Beat)* I'll think about it.

(THE SHERIFF *takes off his watch and hands it to him.*)

SHERIFF: You do that. Meantime, just so there's no confusion. Nine o'clock tonight, Michael. That's it.

(THE SHERIFF *leaves.* MICHAEL *reaches down and flips the switch on the Blue Light. It turns on as the lights fade.*)

Scene Three

(MICHAEL's *house. Late afternoon*)

(MICHAEL *enters in his K-Mart uniform.* PRISCILLA *enters from inside the house.*)

MICHAEL: Hello. Trespassing, I see.

(She folds her arms and studies him for a moment.)

PRISCILLA: There's a man living here. People out on County G have seen him out in the yard, and upstairs at the window.

MICHAEL: Yes and?

PRISCILLA: Simple question: did you go gay? Is that it?

MICHAEL: I didn't go anywhere, Priscilla. That man is the alien.

PRISCILLA: I knew you were going to say that.

MICHAEL: I always said you were sharp, Priscilla.

PRISCILLA: You know, I've been very patient with you. I have not gotten hysterical—which I could have. I have not had you thrown in jail—which I could have. I have very patiently waited while Hank dragged his ass for ten days. Because deep down I knew you wouldn't let anything happen to our little boy. But if this...man has anything at all to do with Billy being gone—I don't care if he's from the moon or Milwaukee, there's going to be serious heck to pay.

(RAY *enters, talking.*)

RAY: I checked all through the attic, but I couldn't find anything else... well, well, well.

MICHAEL: What is going on here? Breaking and entering is a crime, you know.

RAY: We didn't break anything.

MICHAEL: That's not what it means, Ray.

PRISCILLA: All right now.

MICHAEL: He thought it meant that. Didn't you, Ray?

RAY: I'll show you what I meant...!

PRISCILLA: *(To* RAY*)* You go on outside. I'll deal with this.

MICHAEL: You're married to the missing link. You realize that.

RAY: If I wasn't so darned even-tempered, I'd have to have it out with you.

PRISCILLA: Ray, go home. I want to talk to Michael.

RAY: Oh no. He ain't gettin' away so easy this time.

MICHAEL: Get away with what?

RAY: *(To* PRISCILLA*)* Go on, show him.

PRISCILLA: It's fine, Ray, really. Just leave us alone.

RAY: Go on, show him what you found.

*(*PRISCILLA *produces a fistful of makeup in her hand.)*

RAY: Make-up—for girls. Now that's kinky, I don't care what you say.

MICHAEL: He wanted make-up to cover the green skin if he went out.

RAY: He's some kinda kinky guy you met, and now you're co-habitating.

MICHAEL: He's from another planet!

RAY: Which one?

PRISCILLA: Ray, please...

RAY: Which planet? Don't think about it now. Which one?

MICHAEL: I...

RAY: Mars? Jupiter?

MICHAEL: ...I don't know.

RAY: You don't know what planet he's from.

MICHAEL: No.

PRISCILLA: Ray...

RAY: You ever ask?

MICHAEL: No.

PRISCILLA: Ray, listen to me...

RAY: You never once thought to ask.

MICHAEL: No!

RAY: So you're shacked up with this guy, but you don't even know what planet he's from. Don't you want to know the kinda person you're having relations with? Huh? Mike?

PRISCILLA: Ray, go away. Now!

RAY: Fine. You want to side with the uh, what-do-you-call, 'promiscuous homosexual agenda' here, you go right ahead. But you better know one thing. Every item on the shelf has got a price. Every last one. And that goes for both o' youse. *(He exits.)*

PRISCILLA: I didn't come here to snoop. *(She follows RAY as far as the exit, watching to make sure he's gone.)*

MICHAEL: Well, you did a pretty good job of it.

PRISCILLA: Michael, I'm pregnant. *(Pause)* I missed my period last weekend, so I took the home test and I...I don't know what to do!

MICHAEL: Well, Priscilla, it can't be that bad. I mean, you've got Ray...

PRISCILLA: It's not Ray's.

MICHAEL: How do you know?

PRISCILLA: Believe me, I know.

MICHAEL: So you've been—stepping out...

PRISCILLA: No! Once. Ten days ago. Right after Billy... *(She looks at him, doesn't want to start a fight.)* ...was gone.

MICHAEL: Oh, really nice timing.

PRISCILLA: I was vulnerable! I was depressed and angry and very lonely. And this...person came along and made me feel like it was all okay. I don't know. It was like...magic. I can't explain. Michael, please, I'm coming to you because you're the only one I didn't think would judge.

MICHAEL: Who is he?

PRISCILLA: I don't know.

MICHAEL: You don't know his name?

PRISCILLA: He came into the bar one day, and one thing // led to another and I—

MICHAEL: *(Overlapping at //)* Came into the bar ...?!

PRISCILLA: Yes.

MICHAEL: The day after Billy—?

PRISCILLA: I was confused, Michael. I felt so isolated. I was raw. He started quoting that Ernest Hemingway thing at me—for whom the bell tolls, that thing—and that's all I remember, basically.

MICHAEL: That's John Donne, Priscilla.

PRISCILLA: Whoever—I fell for it. He sort of reminded me of you, in a way.

MICHAEL: Me?!

PRISCILLA: You, but not you. Better than you. Different. Anyway we spent most the afternoon together. It was very strange, with Ray right there, passed out the whole time. But somehow, very right. The entire time I was with this man, I could feel myself changing, inside, deep inside— being rearranged, becoming the person I was always meant to be. I even stopped worrying about Billy. I didn't stop thinking about him, but I stopped worrying.

Then we said goodbye finally. He said he couldn't give me his number. I understood, of course. He never actually said he'd call, but of course I assumed—like the dupe that I am. *(She unconsciously touches her stomach.)* I have to have it, Michael. You know me, I couldn't not have it.

MICHAEL: What if I could find him for you?

PRISCILLA: What are you saying?

MICHAEL: I know who he is.

PRISCILLA: Well, who?

MICHAEL: No, I don't think I'd better tell you.

PRISCILLA: Why not?

MICHAEL: It's the...him.

PRISCILLA: Michael, we've had our problems. But I was always under the impression that when push came to shove we were still friends—that I could at least talk to you.

Now listen to me: there are no aliens! Aliens did not take Billy. You are not living with an alien. An alien did not get me pregnant! This is the real world Michael, and in the real world there are no such things as aliens! Or angels! Or flying! Now if you have a shred of human compassion in you, I'm begging you—stop running away from reality, have a little gratitude for the fact that I left you, and for once in your life help me!!

MICHAEL: Oh my god.

PRISCILLA: What?

MICHAEL: *(An epiphany)* I just realized—I don't love you, Priscilla.

PRISCILLA: Well good.

MICHAEL: I don't love you.

PRISCILLA: I'm very glad.

MICHAEL: *(Clutching her back)* I mean, I really don't love you.

PRISCILLA: Michael, I know that. Let go of me.

MICHAEL: I haven't loved you for years. I thought I did—all this time. Because there you were...so beautiful, so smart—don't roll your eyes— you are. I couldn't believe that someone like you couldn't be what I wanted. I kept thinking to myself—underneath all these intense feelings of hostility, she must be the woman for me. But now all of a sudden, it's so clear: I don't love you! I only loved what I wanted you to be! And I couldn't stand to see you go because I always thought somehow, someday you'd be that person. But you won't. I know that now! And I really don't love you!

PRISCILLA: Well, I...I don't love you too.

MICHAEL: I know. Isn't it great?

(He embraces her and she responds. They hold tight for a moment.)

PRISCILLA: Great. Now where is he?

(THE ALIEN has entered through the front door during the above, behind Priscilla's back. Michael points to him. She turns to see him. He smiles at her, touching her on the arm.)

ALIEN: Greetings earthling!

PRISCILLA: Eek! *(She grabs MICHAEL.)*

PRISCILLA: You're...you're—it's you.

ALIEN: Yes.

PRISCILLA: *(To MICHAEL)* You weren't making it up.

MICHAEL: No.

PRISCILLA: You were telling the truth. The whole time.

MICHAEL: Yes.

PRISCILLA: You don't have Billy.

MICHAEL: No.

PRISCILLA: He has Billy.

MICHAEL: No, the ones in the ship—they have Billy. This one's a busboy.

PRISCILLA: You're a busboy?

ALIEN: Yeah.

MICHAEL: He's an AWOL alien busboy.

PRISCILLA: *(Takes a step towards* THE ALIEN*)* You...asshole!

ALIEN: Is she talking to me?

MICHAEL: My guess is yeah.

PRISCILLA: *(Approaching him now)* Where's my son?

ALIEN: *(Backing away)* He's in the ship. He'll be back soon.

PRISCILLA: *(Pursuing)* Soon isn't good enough, mister. I've been very patient about this.

ALIEN: I know. You've been wonderful.

PRISCILLA: You get those friends of yours on the horn and you get my boy back.

ALIEN: I can't.

PRISCILLA: Sorry—don't understand "can't". Not familiar with that word.

ALIEN: It means not able!

PRISCILLA: *(Grabs him and puts him in a arm lock)* Oh really? And what if I took off your left arm and beat you over your head with the bloody stump? How would that affect your "not able"?

ALIEN: Michael, help me. She's hurting me!

MICHAEL: Priscilla, I already tried this. He can't.

*(*PRISCILLA *lets go of the* ALIEN.*)*

ALIEN: What did I do? *(To* MICHAEL*)* Did I hurt her in some way?

MICHAEL: Yes—you loved her, you left her, and you didn't call.

PRISCILLA: You might have told me you weren't human. That would be the considerate thing to do before sleeping with someone.

ALIEN: It never occurred to me. I didn't think it was important.

PRISCILLA: I'm having a baby, you jerk!

ALIEN: You are? I am?

*(*MICHAEL *nods yes.)*

ALIEN: I'm going to be a father?

PRISCILLA: Yes!

ALIEN: *(To* MICHAEL*)* I'm going to be a father.

MICHAEL: Yeah, I heard.

ALIEN: *(To* PRISCILLA, *warmly)* I'm going to be a father!

PRISCILLA: Don't give me the warm glow treatment, mister. You have reduced me to fodder for those magazines at the check-out line. Well I am not going to be just another notch in your ray gun, buddy!

ALIEN: Listen, you had something to do with it too.

PRISCILLA: You sweet-talked me.

ALIEN: You wanted to be sweet-talked.

PRISCILLA: You took advantage of my vulnerability.

ALIEN: I soothed your raw, anxious nerves. I made you feel better.

PRISCILLA: Sure—then you dumped me.

ALIEN: I was confused. It took me a few days.

PRISCILLA: Ten. But who's counting.

ALIEN: I had a lot to figure out. But I finally did. Michael can tell you, I was just about to come to you. I even had him buy make-up, so you wouldn't be too startled.

PRISCILLA: So you were going to go on pretending to be something you weren't.

ALIEN: You mean from earth?

PRISCILLA: Your skin looked normal in the bar.

ALIEN: Wait a second. This is that 'race' thing, isn't it. That's very important to you. I read up on it.

MICHAEL: You read something?

ALIEN: Fine, it was a video.

PRISCILLA: This is not about 'race.'

ALIEN: Look, you have to understand—nobody else in the entire galaxy has even heard of this concept. We figure it's got to be some kind of weird psychological quirk you people have to keep life complicated and difficult. Almost as if you didn't really want to be happy.

PRISCILLA: I'd love to be happy. I just want to know what I'm sleeping with.

ALIEN: Well, wouldn't we all. It's a good thing I happen to be the right gender for you. Otherwise you wouldn't even give me a second look.

PRISCILLA: *(To* MICHAEL*)* He's kidding, right?

ALIEN: And the amazing thing is that you're able to find somebody you actually like after you're done eliminating all the people you've convinced yourself aren't right for you.

But where I come from, we take a slightly simpler approach: you find somebody you like, and everything else—well, you work around it.

And I like you. Even if you are different. Because even in the ways that we're different, there are some pretty great ways that we seem to, sort of, uh...complement each other.

PRISCILLA: You make it sound so easy.

ALIEN: It is easy. This, anyway. Things that are really complicated, well—what can you do. But things that are simple, why not leave them simple?

(She looks at MICHAEL.*)*

MICHAEL: He's got a point.

PRISCILLA: You're an alien.

ALIEN: *(Sympathetically)* I know.

PRISCILLA: It's very hard to get past that.

ALIEN: *(Again)* I know.

PRISCILLA: You're green.

ALIEN: And you're pink.

PRISCILLA: Besides which, you're going to get back on your spaceship, and go flying off into the wild blue yonder.

ALIEN: Well, I've been thinking about that. I really don't like it with them. I mean, I love them. But I can't stand them.

And besides, now I've got a very good reason to stay. *(He goes to her.)*

PRISCILLA: I'm a married woman.

ALIEN: Get a divorce.

PRISCILLA: Right. Okay.

But I'm not going to marry you. I'm on a very bad trend and I want to break it.

(They start to kiss.)

PRISCILLA: What kind of baby am I going to have?

ALIEN: The usual. Part you, part me.

PRISCILLA: Will he be tinted?

ALIEN: Don't worry—you and I are not the first—and they always get your skin color. I realize that's important.

PRISCILLA: You make me sound prejudiced.

ALIEN: Yes, but I like you anyway.

(They kiss. MICHAEL *sighs happily.)*

ALIEN: Hold on! Hold on!...

PRISCILLA: What's wrong?

ALIEN: Wait a second...

PRISCILLA: What is it?

ALIEN: Quiet please! I'm getting a...They're on their way!

PRISCILLA: What?

ALIEN: The ship. It's coming back!

(Lights out.)

Scene Four

(The bar. RAY *is behind the bar, eyeing the barrel of the shotgun.* THE SHERIFF *is reading* Anna Karenina. *Out of the corner of his eye, he catches* RAY *aiming the gun at him.)*

SHERIFF: God darn it, Ray. Point that thing some other way, would you?

RAY: It ain't loaded.

SHERIFF: Yeah, but it's a good bet you are. Now put it the heck down. I'm trying to concentrate here.

*(*RAY *lowers the gun, but hangs on to it.)*

RAY: He could be halfway to Canada by now and you're busy readin' Tchaikovsky there.

*(*THE SHERIFF *indulgently closes the book, but keeps a finger at his place.)*

SHERIFF: What time is it?

RAY: 8:52.

SHERIFF: You didn't even look. It's not that late.

RAY: I guarantee, it's 8:52. I got a very accurate internal clock. Real fishermen all got very accurate internal clocks.

SHERIFF: They do?

RAY: Yup.

SHERIFF: Why is that?

RAY: So you be sure to make last call.

SHERIFF: Anyhow, it's not nine yet. *(He starts to open the book again.)*

RAY: You know, a lot of us do lousy jobs we don't like.

SHERIFF: *(Not looking up)* I realize that.

RAY: Don't mean we shirk our duty.

SHERIFF: I'm not shirking. I'm stalling. Check your watch. Go ahead.

(RAY checks his watch.)

RAY: It's 8:54.

SHERIFF: You're internal clock is slow.

RAY: No. The watch runs fast.

SHERIFF: Either way, it's still not time.

RAY: Well how much longer you gonna give him, for cryin' outside?

SHERIFF: Mind your own business.

(He opens the book again and starts to read. RAY provokes him ...)

RAY: What do you think—some alien spaceship's gonna bring Billy back?

SHERIFF: Possibly.

RAY: You don't believe in no spaceship.

SHERIFF: I believe in Michael. Anyway, a few hours won't make much difference one way or the other.

RAY: No, 'less he's heading for Canada.

SHERIFF: He's not heading for Canada.

RAY: You don't think so, huh?

SHERIFF: No, I don't think so. He's going to do the right thing and bring Billy back.

RAY: Yah?

SHERIFF: Yah.

RAY: You don't sound too sure.

SHERIFF: I'm pretty darn sure.

(Pause)

RAY: 8:56.

SHERIFF: *(Reading)* So?

RAY: So hows 'bout a drink?

SHERIFF: No thanks.

RAY: Come on, just you and me. Nobody's going to know.

SHERIFF: Can't drink on duty. Same as you, Ray.

RAY: Well, it ain't same as me tonight.

(RAY *fixes a drink behind the bar.* THE SHERIFF *looks up, impressed.*)

SHERIFF: I thought the uh...management didn't like that.

RAY: That was the old management. New management don't care what I do.

SHERIFF: What are you talkin'?

RAY: I fired the old management this afternoon.

SHERIFF: How'd she take it?

RAY: She don't know yet. But I figured it only made sense since her and me were gettin' a divorce.

SHERIFF: You're getting divorced?

RAY: Yup.

SHERIFF: How did she take that?

RAY: She don't know that yet either. Gonna tell her when she gets home tonight. She's gonna miss those long nights of pleasure, but she'll get over it. Say what you like about Priscilla, she knows the price of peanuts.

(*He takes a long drink.* THE SHERIFF *opens his book.*)

RAY: What is that thing, anyhow?

SHERIFF: See for yourself.

(THE SHERIFF *hands him the book.* RAY *takes it and turns to the first page.*)

RAY: "Happy families are all alike; every unhappy family is unhappy in its own way." (*He riffles through to the end of the book, then exchanges a significant look at* THE SHERIFF.)

SHERIFF: That's hittin' it square on the nose, ain't it hey.

RAY: Yah.

SHERIFF: What time is it?

RAY: 9:00.

SHERIFF: It's time.

(THE SHERIFF *officiously heads for the door, followed by* RAY *who begins to take the shotgun with him.*)

SHERIFF: And no duck hunting.

(RAY *leaves the gun on the bar and they exit.*)

(*Lights fade.*)

Scene Five

(The clearing in the woods)

(Twilight. THE ALIEN *and* PRISCILLA *enter.* MICHAEL *lags behind a bit.)*

ALIEN: We're here. This is it.

(They all stop. THE ALIEN *checks the sky.)*

PRISCILLA: Any sign?

ALIEN: Not yet. They're still pretty far out.

PRISCILLA: How you do know?

ALIEN: They send messages. I have this doohickey.

PRISCILLA: You mean like a radio?

ALIEN: Not really.

MICHAEL: Don't even try, okay?

PRISCILLA: But they're bringing Billy back, right? For sure.

ALIEN: Of course. That's why they're coming. And also—well, you know—

PRISCILLA: What?

ALIEN: They'll be looking for me. But I'm not going. Not if I can help it.

PRISCILLA: Not if you...! You promised.

MICHAEL: It wouldn't be the first time he changed the story.

ALIEN: *(To* PRISCILLA*)* But they really are coming this time.

MICHAEL: Let's face it—you're the little alien who cried ship.

ALIEN: I couldn't help it last time. They went back for more tests.

PRISCILLA: Tests? What kind of tests?!

ALIEN: All different kinds. But the worst ones are those tests where you have a ship going from Alpha Centauri to Aldebaran at thirty light years an hour, and another ship coming from Aldebaran to Alpha Centauri at sixty light years an hour, and when do they pass each other?

PRISCILLA: They're giving him math tests?

ALIEN: I never said they were nice. *(To* MICHAEL*)* And they can't change their minds this time because they're low on gas. They'll only just get back home as it is.

MICHAEL: You see? You say things like that and we're supposed to believe you. Spaceships don't run on gas.

ALIEN: How would you know?

(The ship passes by overhead—noises and lights.)

ALIEN: Okay? Good enough? Now look—I don't want to go back. I want to stay.

PRISCILLA: Well, what are we going to do?

ALIEN: I don't know. The thing is that they can be very determined.

PRISCILLA: What does that mean?

ALIEN: If they want me back, they have their ways.

PRISCILLA: Well, we're going to have to hide you.

ALIEN: They'll look and they'll find me.

PRISCILLA: What if we took you back and put you in the basement? Or the silo at Michael's barn. Or an old fallout shelter! Would that work?

ALIEN: If I'm missing, they'll find me. Believe me.

PRISCILLA: *(To* MICHAEL*)* Well, think of something!

MICHAEL: What if they didn't think you were missing? What if we put somebody else on the ship, even if it wasn't you...I bet they'd just close the doors and take off.

ALIEN: That's it ? !

PRISCILLA: Michael...you can't...

MICHAEL: Yes, I can. *(To* THE ALIEN*)* Can't I.

ALIEN: Absolutely!

PRISCILLA: Michael, this is out of the question.

MICHAEL: No, don't you see? It's the answer to the question. I've finally got someplace to go.

PRISCILLA: But you don't know what you're doing! Not in a spaceship!

ALIEN: It's easy. Just one, crucial thing: serve from the left, take from the right.

MICHAEL: I'm not getting on that ship so I can be a busboy.

PRISCILLA: You're not getting on that ship, period.

ALIEN: Okay, here's what you do. Right after take off, go straight to the main control room and tell them what's up.

MICHAEL: Okay.

PRISCILLA: What if they don't like it? What if they get angry?

ALIEN: They don't really get angry. Condescending yes, but not angry. Anyway, they'll like Michael.

MICHAEL: You think so?

ALIEN: A lot more than they ever liked me. Just get them going on Beethoven or something.

PRISCILLA: They know Beethoven?

ALIEN & MICHAEL: They loooove Beethoven.

MICHAEL: Okay, so where's the control room?

ALIEN: Well, when you get inside, you take a right. Not your first right, that's the bathroom. The second right, it's a four way.

MICHAEL: The second right.

ALIEN: And you go down the corridor about...I don't know...I'm really bad at distances, but let's say a hundred feet.

MICHAEL: A hundred feet.

ALIEN: Maybe a hundred fifty.

MICHAEL: A hundred fifty.

ALIEN: Wait a second! There's a water fountain. On your left is a water fountain.

MICHAEL: Water fountain on the left.

ALIEN: If you get to that, you went too far. So go back about twenty feet and take a right.

MICHAEL: Okay, second right, then right again.

ALIEN: Well, no. I mean, if you went past it and got to the water fountain and had to go back, then it's a right. Right?

MICHAEL: Right.

ALIEN: But if you get it right the first time, then it's a left.

MICHAEL: Right.

ALIEN: Left. And you're there! Simple.

PRISCILLA: You're going to get lost.

ALIEN: You're going to make it.

PRISCILLA: You can't just go to another planet. People don't do things like that.

MICHAEL: Maybe they should.

PRISCILLA: Michael, there are problems. I'll grant you that. You have a hard time fitting in, but this is your planet and you're staying right where you are!

MICHAEL: Everyday people are born in the wrong time or the wrong place. It's very common, it's just that with me it's a little more drastic. I can't go to another century, Priscilla, but I can do this.

PRISCILLA: These are unusual circumstances. You're all worked up. You haven't thought it through.

MICHAEL: I think about this every day of my life!
Priscilla, don't you see? I suffer from culture shock in the world of my birth. I'm like a refugee, a temporary resident, waiting for my visa application to go through so I can go home to where I belong. Now all of a sudden, somebody hands me a passport and all my papers, and says 'now or never.' I'll miss you but I have to go. I want to go.
And not just for me, Priscilla. For you too. This is the one, best gift I'll ever give you. He's perfect for you. He's decent and honest and loves you for who you are, and he'll love Billy just the same way. And best of all he wants to be here.
And let's face it, I love Billy, and he loves me. But only because he's the most patient boy on earth.
Take the gift, Priscilla. It's the only thing I've ever given you that you really wanted.

(A bright light from offstage, sounds of a spaceship landing.)

ALIEN: They're coming down!

PRISCILLA: Michael, I'm worried. I can't help it.

MICHAEL: I'll send you a sign. How's that?

PRISCILLA: What kind of sign?

MICHAEL: I don't know. A signal. When you get it, it means everything's fine. Okay?
Good bye.

(She grabs him and they embrace.)

MICHAEL: And uh—you too. (He embraces THE ALIEN and turns to go.)

ALIEN: Michael. Thank you.

(They lock gazes for a split second.)

(The ship lands.)

(THE ALIEN ducks behind a log and Michael turns back to the ship as BILLY appears.)

BILLY: Dad! Mom!

(BILLY runs to them. They have a three-way embrace.)

MICHAEL: Are you all right?

BILLY: I'm fine.

PRISCILLA: Don't let me go. Are you all right? Talk to me.

BILLY: I'm fine.

PRISCILLA: Did they hurt you?

BILLY: No. But those math tests were really hard.

MICHAEL: How did you do?

BILLY: I aced 'em.

MICHAEL: That's my boy!

(The lights flash and swirl for a moment, then stop.)

(MICHAEL draws BILLY to him. PRISCILLA knowingly retreats.)

MICHAEL: Listen, we've only got a second. There's been a...a kind of a change in plans. I'm not staying here with you.

BILLY: What do you mean?

MICHAEL: You see, they left one of their own. He's taking my place on earth....

BILLY: ...and you're taking his place on the ship.

MICHAEL: Billy, I just...can you understand? I want it to be clear—we won't ever see each other again.

BILLY: Wow—that is kind of a drag.

MICHAEL: It's a really huge drag.

(They embrace.)

BILLY: But Dad—wait a second! Once you get inside, they'll give you this doohickey. It goes right here in your tooth. *(He indicates.)* People send you their thoughts, and you can send yours too!

MICHAEL: You got a two-way?

BILLY: Oh yeah—if they like you, they make it a two-way.

(In the background, THE ALIEN reacts.)

BILLY: So when you get yours and I have mine, we can always be in contact with each other—anytime we want, just by thinking!

MICHAEL: Wow.

BILLY: Yeah, cool—huh?

MICHAEL: But Billy, can you understand why I have to do this?

BILLY: Oh yeah.

MICHAEL: You can.

BILLY: It's just like on this one Star Trek. These two guys were in the wrong universes from the beginning, and they had to get back to the universe they belonged in, even if that wasn't where they came from. Because the other universe was, like, where they belonged.

MICHAEL: That's right. That's it.

BILLY: You see? You always said Star Trek was crap, but sometimes it's just like life.

(Lights swirl and flash again, this time they don't stop.)

MICHAEL: I love you. *(He grabs* BILLY *and draws him close.)*

BILLY: I love you too, Dad. You better get going.

MICHAEL: I'm really going to miss you, Billy. I'll miss you a whole planet's worth.

BILLY: Me too, Dad.

(They embrace once more then pull away. BILLY *starts to exit.)*

MICHAEL: Mind your mother. Unless you really think she's wrong. In which case, try to make the ethical choice.

BILLY: 'kay, I will!

*(*BILLY *crosses to* PRISCILLA. *The lights flash, whirl, become blinding as* MICHAEL *disappears into them.)*

*(*THE ALIEN *emerges from behind the log and takes his place at* PRISCILLA's *side.)*

ALIEN: Hello.

BILLY: Hi.

ALIEN: I'm in love with your mother.

PRISCILLA: I hope that's all right.

BILLY: It's okay by me.

PRISCILLA: Really? You don't mind?

BILLY: He's got to be better than Ray, that's for sure.
    Besides, from what they said about him on the ship— *(To* THE ALIEN*)* —you sound great.

(They do a 'special' handshake. Spaceships lights and noises off stage as it starts to rise. They all look towards it.)

(Softly, in the background, we hear music rising....)

(RAY and THE SHERIFF enter at a run. RAY still has his beer with him. They stop, awestruck at the rising ship.)

SHERIFF: Michael!... Billy!... Michael...

RAY: ...dang!

BILLY: Hey, do you hear that?

PRISCILLA: What the heck is that?

(The music rises now. It's Beethoven's Seventh Symphony, *end of the First Movement.)*

ALIEN & BILLY: Beethoven!

PRISCILLA: It's your father. It's his sign!

BILLY: They sure looove their Beethoven.

ALIEN: There he goes!

(Their heads slowly turn upwards to follow the ship over their heads, until they end up facing out to the audience. The music rises to a crescendo.)

SHERIFF: I told him to think about relocating, but holy cripes!

PRISCILLA: Good bye Michael!

BILLY: Good bye Dad!

RAY: And don't come crawlin' back, either!

ALIEN: Bye bye! Bye bye!

EVERYONE: *(But RAY)* Good bye! Good bye!

(Their hands reach out towards the audience to wave good bye as the music climaxes and the lights fade to black.)

END OF PLAY

IN THE WESTERN GARDEN

Part Two of IN THE WESTERN GARDEN was originally presented as a one act in the Ensemble Studio Theatre's Marathon of One Act Plays '95 under the title WATER AND WINE. The cast and creative contributors were:

GIONVANNI .... Ed Setrakian
ENRICO .... Justin Theroux
GIULIANO .... Frank Biancamano
BUONARROTI .... Chris Ceraso

Director .... Nicholas Martin
Stage manager .... Greg W Brevoort

Part Three was presented under the title IN THE WESTERN GARDEN in Marathon '99. The cast and creative contributors were:

SALLY .... Peggity Price
GENE .... Robert Hogan
ALAN .... Rob Morrow
LEONARD .... David Margulies

Director .... Judy Minor
Stage manager .... Paul Powell

PRODUCTION NOTE

IN THE WESTERN GARDEN can be performed according to the following casting scheme:

First Actor: GIOVANNI (Part Two)
GENE (Part Three)

Second Actor: ENRICO (Part Two)
ALAN (Part Three)

Third Actor: BUONARROTI (Part Two)
DENNIS (Part One)

Fourth Actor: GIULIANO (Part Two)
LEONARD (Part Three)

The Actress: SALLY (Part Three)
ALICE (Part One)

NOTE

Though IN THE WESTERN GARDEN was conceived as a single, complete piece, it does seem an overstatement to call it a "play." It's really three plays, of course, and while each play may be performed separately, together they constitute a single work, a trilogy. Most trilogies we know are connected either by an ongoing story, or by a group of characters, or at least by a single setting. IN THE WESTERN GARDEN has none of these. Instead it finds its roots in ancient Greek drama, in which the trilogies were often constructed around nothing more than a common theme.

The piece is about more than just its overall architectural ideas, but it may help in understanding IN THE WESTERN GARDEN to know something of the large, cohering principles that informed its construction. The function of Part One (THE ROTHKO ROOM) is a reflection of its own subject: it is itself a 'portal' into the other two plays. It serves as a signal that the evening is not merely about "art" but about the idea that, on the one hand art is an utterly personal expression of the artist, and on the other hand it means nothing without a viewer to make sense of it for him- or herself.

Part Two (WATER AND WINE) deals with our Western classical ideas of art, and that the passion to create cannot be denied in a Michelangelo anymore than in an obscure peasant farmer. The play may seem to ask who is the "real" artist, but is in fact about whether the flame of passion—if it is real—can ever be snuffed out. And finally in Part Three (LEVELS OF PERCEPTION) we arrive in our modern world, in which the struggle is now between those who believe that everything that can be said has already been said, and those who believe that to say it again, with passion, is our only worthy answer to the void.

The piece is a journey, then, if not one of plot then one of the mind. Even so, I do like to think that, while there are different *people* in each play, there are in fact *characters* that can be followed from one play to the other. To say which would be intrusive, and so I leave that discovery to you, the reader, and the audience.

"It is closing time in the gardens of the west, and from now on an artist will be judged only by the resonance of his solitude or the quality of his despair."

Cyril Connolly, *The Unquiet Grave*

Part One
THE ROTHKO ROOM

(The Tate Gallery, London. The "Rothko room." We see large canvasses by Rothko—the Seagram murals.)

(A low bench in the middle of the room)

(Lights up)

(Two figures occupy the space. ALICE, a woman approximately in her forties, and DENNIS, who is about the same age, though perhaps a little younger. They are each studying a different painting.)

(Lights down)

(Lights up again. ALICE and DENNIS again, this time studying different paintings.)

(Lights down)

(Lights up again. ALICE and DENNIS study different paintings again.)

(Lights down)

(Lights up. They are in yet a new position, with their backs more or less to each other. They each start to back up a bit to get a better view of the canvas. They gently graze each other.)

DENNIS: Oh! Sorry...

ALICE: It's all right....

DENNIS: Didn't see you there...

ALICE: It's quite all right....

(He stands aside. They both look at the paintings. She sits on the bench, removes her shoes. He glances her way. She is looking at the painting. He looks at it also. A pause for thought...)

DENNIS: They're all portals.

ALICE: Excuse me?

DENNIS: Doors. Windows. Archways, stage curtains. That's what gives the room cohesion. They're each a form of entrance, a gateway into...something.

ALICE: *(Letting it register, but not entirely sure yet)* Yes...

DENNIS: Obvious, when you think about it.

ALICE: Obvious but...subtle.

DENNIS: Well, you wouldn't want "doorway" written under every one.

ALICE: I should say.

DENNIS: Do you have a favorite?

ALICE: Uh...well...those two I think—down at the end.

(He turns to look. We can see them also.)

DENNIS: *(Disappointed)* Oh.

ALICE: What.

DENNIS: Those two—they're the only ones that are....

ALICE: Yes?

DENNIS: ...not portals.

ALICE: Oh.

DENNIS: They're ground plans.

ALICE: *(Looking at them)* How can you tell?

DENNIS: Well, you see—you're not looking *through* something. You're looking *down*. From above. Bird's eye view. Like the site of an excavation. That's the outline of the building there. See?

ALICE: *(Dawning...)* Oh...yes. All right.

DENNIS: *(Leaving these behind)* But the rest of them, these—they're all portals to another place.

ALICE: *(Taking them in)* Yes. Well, I can certainly see that. Yes.

(He sits down next to her.)

DENNIS: *(Modestly)* Standard interpretation.

ALICE: Really.

DENNIS: Oh sure.

ALICE: I never would have thought of it— .

DENNIS: I read it in a book.

ALICE: Very informative. Thank you. That was quite helpful. Thank you.

DENNIS: The question is, what place? Portals to where?

ALICE: *(Surprised; she looks back to the paintings again.)* I don't know.

DENNIS: One doesn't know, does one.

ALICE: No...

DENNIS: Almost as if he didn't want us to know.

ALICE: *(Still looking at them)* No...

DENNIS: As if he wanted it a secret.

ALICE: *(Confirmed now)* Yes.

DENNIS: Not to know.

ALICE: Not literally anyway.

DENNIS: Right, exactly.

ALICE: Where do you think they go?

(He looks at her as if surprised by the question, as if seeing her now for the first time. He almost studies her.)

DENNIS: Where have you been?

ALICE: Well I...what do you mean?

DENNIS: Where are you going?

ALICE: Nowhere special.

DENNIS: No particular destination?

ALICE: Well...here, I suppose. This *became* my destination. Doesn't that ever happen to you. You arrive, then you think—yes, this is it.

DENNIS: Interesting.

ALICE: Is it?

DENNIS: Well, you know the story of how *they*... *(The paintings)* ...got here.

ALICE: No.

DENNIS: They were meant as a mural for some restaurant. A famous one, I forget the name, but very famous. In New York City. A commission. But he finishes them and he thinks, "I don't want my paintings looking down on some rich bastards chewing their bloody sirloins." So he returns the commission and he keeps the paintings. For ten years, they sit. Nothing. Then *this* place offers to buy them, and he says "All right, but on one condition: They get their own room, with the lighting just so—like this, very dark, and they all stay together. *It* stays together, the mural, forever."

ALICE: And not a sirloin steak in sight.

DENNIS: So the Gallery says, all right. That's fine. We accept your condition. The paintings arrive from New York, and on that very morning they get a call overseas, from the dealer in New York. That very night, while the paintings were high up over the Atlantic, on their way here—at that very moment, he killed himself.

(He looks at the paintings. She looks at them too, as if for the first time.)

DENNIS: See what I mean?

ALICE: I'm not sure.

DENNIS: It was *his* destination also.

ALICE: Like a letter from a dead man.

(He looks at her for a moment....)

DENNIS: How could you leave like that?

ALICE: Dennis, don't.

DENNIS: Answer me.

ALICE: I didn't leave.

DENNIS: Oh really?

ALICE: Well I'm here, aren't I? I'm here now.

(He looks at her angrily. Then he looks to the painting on the fourth wall for a long moment, silent. She looks at it too. A pause.)

ALICE: If you look long enough, they start to shimmer.

DENNIS: Yes?

ALICE: Vibrate, almost. This one in particular.

(She nods to the fourth wall. He looks at her skeptically.)

ALICE: Go ahead, look.

(He looks. A long pause)

ALICE: Do you see?

DENNIS: ...no.

(Her eyes don't leave the canvas.)

ALICE: Go stand right up next to it.

DENNIS: What do you mean?

ALICE: Eighteen inches is the perfect distance.

(He looks at her skeptically.)

ALICE: That's what *he* says. *(A nod to the painting, indicating she means Rothko.)*

DENNIS: How do you know?

ALICE: It's in the flyer. *(She indicates the museum brochure.)* Go ahead. Go right up to it.

(He stands and walks far downstage, facing the audience. He is inches from the painting.)

ALICE: Give it a moment.

(He continues to look. Another long pause.)

ALICE: Yes?

DENNIS: *(After a moment, still looking. There's a glimmer, but he's still not sure.)* Mmmm.

ALICE: Yes?

DENNIS: *(Suddenly, like a revelation)* Yes.

ALICE: As if there's something behind...something else.

DENNIS: *(Still looking, caught up in the experience)* When did you notice this?

ALICE: I just—I don't know. I found myself watching it and it started to shimmer—

DENNIS: Yes.

ALICE: Tremble almost. And there's nothing but the painting.

DENNIS: ...nothing, no...

ALICE: ...shimmering, vibrating...

DENNIS: ...lambent.

ALICE: Beautiful, but...

(Slight pause)

DENNIS: *(Still looking)* But what?

ALICE: But...not beautiful.

DENNIS: Yes. Beautiful. And...not beautiful. That's exactly it. *(He steps away from the painting, turning to look at her, though he stays where he is.)*

(She starts to put on her shoes.)

DENNIS: You can't go now.

ALICE: That's all I wanted to do. I wanted you to see that.

DENNIS: Wanted me to see what?

ALICE: *(Not really paying attention; struggling to get her shoe on)* That it shimmers. That there's something there.

DENNIS: Yes and what else?

ALICE: What do you mean, what else? What else is there?

DENNIS: But why does it shimmer?

ALICE: I can't explain that.

DENNIS: Then why are you telling me?

ALICE: I'm not telling you. I asked you to look, and you did. You looked, you *saw*.

DENNIS: There's got to be more to it than that. You must know *why*.

ALICE: It shimmers because that's what it does.

DENNIS: And why should it do that?

ALICE: I can't explain.

DENNIS: Because something is on the other side? Because we can see through to the other side?

ALICE: Yes.

DENNIS: Then what is it? What's on the other side?

ALICE: If I could tell you, I would. But there's nothing I could say that would explain. If I could, there wouldn't be any reason for the painting. *(Her shoe is on. She starts to go.)*

DENNIS: This is worse than the fact that you left in the first place. Do you know that?
   Or is it that you just don't you care.

(This cuts. She turns impatiently. She looks at the fourth wall painting, then to DENNIS.)

ALICE: All right, what do you see?

DENNIS: I just told you.

ALICE: Behind that. The reason for all that shimmering.

DENNIS: *(Slight pause; considering)* I don't want to say.

ALICE: Why not?

DENNIS: I don't want to think it.

ALICE: Why not?

DENNIS: Because it's...it's not...it's like you said: it's something...not beautiful.

ALICE: And?

(He looks again.)

DENNIS: It's like the flickering of a candle.

ALICE: So?

DENNIS: Like a flame.

ALICE: And?

DENNIS: And it scares me.

ALICE: It can be frightening, yes.

DENNIS: *(Sarcastically)* Well that's very comforting. Thanks a lot.

(He turns away. She takes a moment to re-consider.)

ALICE: Sunlight.

DENNIS: *(Confused)* ...what? I'm sorry, but I don't....

ALICE: That's the closest way to say it. Sunlight. It's a flame, after all, isn't it. A terrible, blinding burning. But at the same time, quite beautiful. The most beautiful thing there is.

DENNIS: *(Realization)* It's true.

ALICE: Isn't it.

DENNIS: You're right.

ALICE: So in a sense...

DENNIS: Yes.

(Beat. She goes back to the other subject.)

ALICE: It had nothing to do with you.

DENNIS: No, I know that.

ALICE: Do you? Really?

DENNIS: Well, it sometimes feels as though...maybe...I wasn't—oh this is stupid....

ALICE: What?

DENNIS: ...worthy.

ALICE: Well that's all it was. A feeling.
   If you think about it, if you really try to understand—you'll know it was just...I had to go. There wasn't any choice. Yours, mine, anyone's. It was time for me to go. Everyone has their time. I've had mine, you'll have yours.

DENNIS: I was so *angry*. I'm still angry—even now....

ALICE: Of course. Who wouldn't be?

DENNIS: Really? You think?   ·

ALICE: *(Laughing)* Oh please. Furious!

DENNIS: I kept—I just assumed I was somehow...I don't know. A crank of some kind.

ALICE: You're not a crank.
   Well, you are—talking to yourself in galleries after all.

DENNIS: Don't say that.

ALICE: What?

DENNIS: "...talking to myself..." You're here. I know you are.

ALICE: Yes, but imagine what someone would see, if they walked in right now.

(Slight pause)

DENNIS: You know, I wonder.

ALICE: Wonder what?

DENNIS: If I knew that you would be here. Not *knew*, but somehow *felt...*

ALICE: You were ready to see me. That's all.

DENNIS: Ready?

ALICE: You were ready.

DENNIS: But why now? I've missed you so long.

ALICE: Today you were ready. I don't know why. One never knows why. Even *he* doesn't try to tell us why. *(A nod to the painting again, indicating Rothko)*

DENNIS: Do you really have to go?

ALICE: I really think I ought to, now.

DENNIS: Hold my hand, would you?

(She takes his hand. He presses it with his other hand.)

DENNIS: Thank you for...

ALICE: ...making this my destination?

DENNIS: Yes...that's it, isn't it. You were...bidden. And you came.

(She smiles indulgently.)

ALICE: Would you like another minute?

DENNIS: No.

ALICE: You're sure?

DENNIS: I'm going to say goodbye here, now. Better that way.

ALICE: That's very smart. You were always such a smart boy. I worried about my other children when I had to leave. But I never worried about you. You were so young, the youngest. But even then I knew how smart you were. And I knew you'd be fine.

DENNIS: Good bye. *(He presses her hand one more time, then turns to study another painting.)*

ALICE: I think you're wrong about those two, though. I think they're all doors.

(She stays for just a moment, then realizes it's time for her to go—the signal has already been given. She turns silently and exits.)

(He watches her go. Then he sits and studies the painting as the lights fade.)

END OF PART ONE

Part Two
WATER AND WINE

(The dark interior of a vaulted chamber. It is used as the storage room for a vineyard, so there are large wooden vats and an array of bottles—some of them full and corked, others empty.)

(There are two exits, both heavy wooden doors. The first goes to the outside. The second, upstage, leads to a "cellar" which is burrowed into the side of the hill, so you don't have to descend steps to get into it. The cellar door is locked.)

(It is late afternoon on a winter's day. Outside it is cold and rainy. The light is beginning to fail. A single candle is on the table. It brings a warm glow to the otherwise dank room. Also on the table is a bowl of grapes and perhaps some other fruit. But we can hear the wind and the rain whipping against the side of this stone structure, buried half beneath the ground.)

(The year is 1506. We are on a farm on a mountainside, north of Rome on the way to Florence.)

(The door bangs open and GIOVANNI enters. He is in his sixties, but the farmer's life has made him look much older. He has a beard, and is weathered and grey.)

(Behind him will follow ENRICO, in his early twenties. He's handsome and energetic, and very earnest.)

GIOVANNI: Christ! What a day! *(He sees the door is still open.)* Close the door for God's sake!

(ENRICO reaches back and closes the heavy wooden door.)

ENRICO: The rain is good for the grapes.

GIOVANNI: Bad for the old men, though.

ENRICO: By next summer, you'll be happy we had so much. You'll be dancing around the wine press singing songs to the Madonna.

GIOVANNI: If I live that long.

ENRICO: You say that every year.

GIOVANNI: Every year I could die. And I have never danced around any wine presses.
  Light a candle.

ENRICO: It's lit. Liccia must have come down.

GIOVANNI: That's not the only candle we have.

ENRICO: They're expensive, papa.

GIOVANNI: Well, we've got money now, don't we.

ENRICO: Do we?

GIOVANNI: We will as soon as they get here and take a look at it. I think they're going to pay plenty, don't you?

ENRICO: I hope so.

GIOVANNI: Ah well, there you go. Hope. You add faith and charity, and you've got yourself a Beatitude.

ENRICO: Faith, hope, and charity are not Beatitudes.

GIOVANNI: No? What are they?

ENRICO: They're just three good things to have. The greatest of them is charity.

GIOVANNI: Forgive me, I'm an old sinner, I can't keep track.

ENRICO: Just because I go to church and you don't...

GIOVANNI: The last time I went to church Father Niccolo scared me half to death with his sermon.

ENRICO: That was twenty years ago.

GIOVANNI: And look at me, I'm still shaking. He's a fanatic.

ENRICO: Father Niccolo has some good things to say.

GIOVANNI: The only things he has to say are what the old men in Rome tell him to say.

(ENRICO *dismisses him with a wave.*)

ENRICO: You're sacrilegious and disrespectful to the church.

GIOVANNI: You only noticed just now? Where are the candles?

(GIOVANNI *is looking for them in a low cabinet against a wall.*)

ENRICO: One is plenty.

GIOVANNI: You wait and see. Not too long and we'll have lots of candles, some new clothes, maybe a dowry for that sister of yours so someday I won't have to listen to her complain about the work she has to do.

ENRICO: Papa...

GIOVANNI: I'm sorry.

ENRICO: We agreed.

GIOVANNI: Yes, yes. I'm sorry.

ENRICO: Liccia works very hard.

GIOVANNI: God knows she works harder than your mother ever did. Now there was a lazy one.

ENRICO: Papa, that's not nice!

GIOVANNI: It's true!

ENRICO: You don't say that about the dead.

GIOVANNI: You say what's true about the dead and let the dead take care of themselves. Anyway, they're dead. What do they care?

ENRICO: You're a wicked old man.

GIOVANNI: We already know that. And you are young and stupid. So when they get here, you let me do the talking. I plan to get our money's worth out of this little...artifact we've discovered.

(He has found three candles. He sits at the table, and sets about putting them in holders and lighting them.)

ENRICO: Little artifact!?

GIOVANNI: Yes, exactly.

ENRICO: Papa! It's sculpture!

GIOVANNI: I'm not impressed by words, I'm sorry.

ENRICO: Just because you don't understand it—

GIOVANNI: Oh! And you do, I suppose.

ENRICO: No, but I admit it. I'm humble in my ignorance.

GIOVANNI: It's a very pretty piece of stone, I'll give you that. But all this talk about art? That's for the Pope and all those bishops and whatnot who love to stroll around the Vatican gasping at all their lovely belongings. Me, I go into the vineyard every day and do my job. And do you know what? When they sit down to their table in the afternoon, they enjoy a very fine wine because of my work. Wine that in my ignorant opinion is every bit a thing of beauty as any of their fancy art.

ENRICO: Our work.

GIOVANNI: You're right—because the one thing you do know how to do is when to pick the grape. I'll give you that.

ENRICO: Thank you.

GIOVANNI: Not just anyone can time it the way you can. We make good wine because of that. It's a real talent.

ENRICO: Thank you Papa.

GIOVANNI: But as far as this goes—a serious, businesslike exchange of cash, that's all I'm looking for. No elegant talk for me, if you please.

ENRICO: You're a terrible philistine.

GIOVANNI: I don't even know what that is, so it can't possibly bother me that I am one.

ENRICO: It's in the Bible.

GIOVANNI: This explains why I don't know.

ENRICO: Anyway, we'll both do the talking.

GIOVANNI: I don't think we're having this discussion.

ENRICO: Both of us, Papa.

GIOVANNI: You don't know the first thing about business.

ENRICO: And you don't know anything about art.

GIOVANNI: I don't need to know anything.

ENRICO: It wouldn't hurt.

GIOVANNI: I'm the head of this family and I do the business.

ENRICO: You could give something away and not even know it.

GIOVANNI: We've got one item on the block: a statue. We're trying to get two thousand for it. We'll settle for one. I know the difference between one and two. That much business sense I know I have.

ENRICO: Just don't close any deals without checking with me first.

GIOVANNI: I'll see how it goes. (*He goes to the upstage door and tests it. It's locked.*)

ENRICO: Papa...

GIOVANNI: I said I'll see. Now leave it. When does he get here?

ENRICO: I don't know. And it's they.

GIOVANNI: They?

(ENRICO *sits at the table.*)

ENRICO: There are two of them. Buonarroti and a friend of his.

GIOVANNI: Another artist?

ENRICO: I don't know.

GIOVANNI: Maybe a businessman.

ENRICO: Maybe.

GIOVANNI: Maybe someone from the Vatican.

ENRICO: Maybe, I don't know.

GIOVANNI: Maybe from the Pope himself.

ENRICO: I doubt it.

GIOVANNI: Why?

ENRICO: Who knows if His Holiness is even interested?

GIOVANNI: Not interested?! Are you serious?

ENRICO: No one has even seen it yet.

GIOVANNI: But you described it to them in your letter, didn't you? You made that little drawing of it.

ENRICO: I'm sure my drawing looked very simple to people like Buonarroti.

GIOVANNI: I thought it looked very nice.

ENRICO: You did?

GIOVANNI: Yes and I don't like you enough to compliment you if you don't deserve it. That was a good drawing.

ENRICO: Thank you.

(GIOVANNI *goes to him.*)

GIOVANNI: I always thought you could draw a good picture.

ENRICO: Thank you.

GIOVANNI: Who knows? With a little instruction, maybe you could be a real artist.

ENRICO: It takes more than a little instruction. It takes a long time and hard work.

GIOVANNI: Yes, well, you're right—you were always lazy.

ENRICO: I am not lazy!

GIOVANNI: Okay, all right.

ENRICO: You know that you need me here, Papa, and that's all there is to it.

GIOVANNI: I was only saying....

ENRICO: We've been through this a hundred times.

GIOVANNI: If you'd let me get a word in...

ENRICO: Let's just drop it!

(ENRICO *gets up and crosses away from* GIOVANNI, *though he soon realizes he has nowhere to go and ends up floating on the other side of the room.*)

GIOVANNI: I never heard of anyone finding a...a whole statue like this, have you?

ENRICO: No. But we don't get much news way up here.

GIOVANNI: They're always digging up a piece of this, a chunk of that. But a whole statue? In almost the same condition as the day it was finished? That can't be the usual thing.

ENRICO: You may be right. I hope so.

GIOVANNI: You and that hope again.

ENRICO: I'm only saying that I don't know.

GIOVANNI: And not just any old statue, but a great one. I mean, that is one very impressive piece of marble, don't you think? So dramatic. The way they're all tangled up in the snakes like that, struggling to get free. It's pathetic, really, if you think about it. Really, very touching.

ENRICO: You sound like you almost like it.

GIOVANNI: (Indignantly) I do.

ENRICO: I thought you couldn't care less about all that fancy art nonsense.

GIOVANNI: I don't care about all the nonsense. But I like the statue. It's... I don't know. It's good. It's nothing to get excited about it, but it's good. I never said it wasn't good.

ENRICO: You said you weren't impressed by it.

GIOVANNI: I never said such a thing.

ENRICO: You did. You just said it a few minutes ago.

GIOVANNI: You don't listen. I said I wasn't impressed by all the nonsense that goes with it. All the talk, talk, talk. Who wouldn't be impressed by it—the thing itself? You'd have to be blind. Or stupid. What do you take me for anyway, a philistine?

(ENRICO goes to the table with the wine bottles on it.)

ENRICO: I'm going to have a little. How about you?

GIOVANNI: Unlike my son, I try not to drink up the profits.

ENRICO: (Pouring a little) Say when.

GIOVANNI: Well, don't be so cheap for God's sake. I worked hard today.

(ENRICO hands him a cup of wine.)

GIOVANNI: You're not such a bad son.

(There's pounding at the outside door.)

GIOVANNI: It's them.

ENRICO: I'll get it.

GIOVANNI: Don't forget, I do the talking.

(More pounding)

GIOVANNI: Come in! Now be obedient for once in your life.

ENRICO: Yes, Papa.

(Two men enter. The first, BUONARROTI, is about thirty. He is bearded and not very attractive. He is overbearing in his manner, abrupt and arrogant. The second man, GIULIANO DA SANGALLO, is in his forties. He is quite straight-forward, businesslike. They are both very wet and wind-blown.)

GIULIANO: God! The wind on this mountain! I'm out of breath!

GIOVANNI: Bad day out there.

GIULIANO: Terrible!

GIOVANNI: Let me take your cloaks. Enrico, some help here.

GIULIANO: Yes, yes, thank you so much.

(Meanwhile, ENRICO has stepped in to take BUONARROTI's cloak. BUONARROTI's eyes fasten on ENRICO, who manages—barely—to meet the gaze. BUONARROTI's tone is stern and formal.)

BUONARROTI: You didn't tell us it was so far up the hill.

ENRICO: It's a steep climb, yes.

BUONARROTI: Look at this. I'm soaked through.

ENRICO: I'll get you some dry clothes if you like.

BUONARROTI: No, no, don't bother. I'm not staying that long.

GIOVANNI: We thought you might stay for dinner.

BUONARROTI: We have to get back.

GIULIANO: I don't know. Dinner doesn't sound so bad to me.

BUONARROTI: I want to be back in the city tonight.

GIULIANO: We're going to have to eat somewhere.

ENRICO: Yes—please stay. It would be such an honor for us to have you....

BUONARROTI: I'm not staying for dinner!

GIOVANNI: If he doesn't want to stay he doesn't have to.

BUONARROTI: I just want to look at the statue. That's what I came for.

ENRICO: Of course, of course. I only meant that...

BUONARROTI: I know what you meant.

GIOVANNI: We let our guests do what they like.

BUONARROTI: Thank you.

GIOVANNI: You don't want to eat my daughter's cooking, there's nobody here going to force you. Although I have to say, it's very good. My name is DeAngelo. This is my son Enrico.

BUONARROTI: I'm Buonarroti.

(GIULIANO *steps forward to shake hands.*)

GIULIANO: Giuliano Da Sangallo. It's a pleasure. His Holiness would like you to know that he's very pleased you told him first of your discovery.

ENRICO: We knew that he would appreciate the value of a great work like this.

GIOVANNI: And have the money to pay for it.

(GIULIANO *is a little embarrassed by this.*)

GIULIANO: Yes, yes of course.

BUONARROTI: May we see the statue?

GIOVANNI: It's right in there. *(He indicates.)* We put it in the cellar—it's got the only door we can lock.

GIULIANO: Very smart.

BUONARROTI: You didn't tell anyone else about it, did you?

GIOVANNI: We're farmers. Farmers are not idiots.

GIULIANO: Oh he didn't mean that you...

(GIOVANNI *goes to get a candle and a key, lying on the table. He unlocks the cellar door.*)

GIOVANNI: We didn't tell anyone. But I didn't want somebody stumbling in here and getting a look at it before you arrived. It's too important. I think you'll agree.
    Well gentlemen? Care to have a look?

(GIULIANO *and* BUONARROTI *look at each other.*)

BUONARROTI: You go ahead.

GIULIANO: You're not coming?

BUONARROTI: I want to sit for a minute. I've got too many thoughts going around in my head. I won't be able to look at it clearly.

GIULIANO: Well, if that's what you want.

BUONARROTI: I do.

GIOVANNI: All right, then. Come along. Take that candle with you.

(GIULIANO *takes a nearby candle. He and* GIOVANNI *exit.*)

ENRICO: Please, have a seat.

BUONARROTI: Thank you.

ENRICO: You're sure you don't want some dry clothes.

BUONARROTI: They'll only get wet when I go back into the rain.

ENRICO: You really can spend the night if you like.

BUONARROTI: You're very kind. No thank you.

ENRICO: Whatever you want. But I want you to know that we're not just being polite.

BUONARROTI: I understand.

ENRICO: The house is comfortable. The beds are warm and dry. No lice. My sister's cooking really is very good—everybody says so, even my father, and he doesn't give out many compliments. I don't understand why you'd want to go back tonight in the rain. It'll be dark soon, too.

BUONARROTI: Maybe I like the dark.

(*This stops* ENRICO *short. He turns away vaguely until his eye falls on the wine bottles.*)

ENRICO: Would you like a glass of wine?

BUONARROTI: Is it your own?

ENRICO: We grow the grapes right out there, on the hillside.

BUONARROTI: I'll try a cup.

(ENRICO *pours two cups.*)

ENRICO: I think we make a good wine here. It's light. But with a good body. (*He hands* BUONARROTI *the cup.*) But you tell me.

(BUONARROTI *drinks it down.*)

BUONARROTI: It's fine.

ENRICO: You barely tasted it.

BUONARROTI: I thought it was fine.

ENRICO: You can't tell when you drink it that fast.

BUONARROTI: I can tell.

ENRICO: Then you don't really care about good wine.

BUONARROTI: You're right, I don't. Now if you don't mind, leave me alone for a minute.

ENRICO: To clear your head.

BUONARROTI: Yes.

ENRICO: The way a wine drinker clears his palate, right? So that you're ready to have the experience.

BUONARROTI: That's right.

ENRICO: That's the only thing that's important to you.

BUONARROTI: Yes.

ENRICO: Sometimes, I draw. Papa tells me I'm very good.

BUONARROTI: For a man who doesn't hand out many compliments, he seems to do it rather often.

ENRICO: I might have gone to Florence to study.

BUONARROTI: Why didn't you?

ENRICO: I thought I should stay on the farm. My father needed the help.

BUONARROTI: We all make choices.

ENRICO: The drawing of the statue that we sent you. Did you bring it?

BUONARROTI: Yes.

ENRICO: May I see it?

BUONARROTI: It's in the cloak. Probably soaked through.

(ENRICO goes to the cloak, rummages through the pockets, and produces a rolled piece of paper. He spreads it on the table.)

ENRICO: Do you mind?

BUONARROTI: Mind?

ENRICO: Giving me a critique?

BUONARROTI: You drew this?

ENRICO: Yes.

BUONARROTI: It's not bad.

ENRICO: Do you think?

BUONARROTI: You must practice.

ENRICO: I do, in my spare time. In the winter, mostly. When the weather is like this.

BUONARROTI: I meant you *ought* to practice. More.

ENRICO: Oh.

BUONARROTI: The modeling of the flesh is abrupt, here. You see? You can bring out the sense of muscle, of weight. Don't pass over it as though it isn't there. It is there. Acknowledge it.

ENRICO: I see. Anything else?

BUONARROTI: That's all.

ENRICO: That's your only criticism?

BUONARROTI: Yes.

ENRICO: You're very kind.

BUONARROTI: No I'm not.

ENRICO: Then you really mean it. You think I have talent.

BUONARROTI: I don't know what talent is. You can draw.

ENRICO: Enough to go to Florence? To study?

BUONARROTI: I have no idea.

ENRICO: Well, if you don't know, who does?

BUONARROTI: You want to make it a matter of talent. I'm only saying that I don't know if talent is so important. There's a lot that goes into being an artist besides talent. Personality. Luck. Skill...

ENRICO: But you said I had skill.

BUONARROTI: There's skill and there's technique.

ENRICO: But that's what I would learn if I studied, wouldn't I?

BUONARROTI: I suppose so.

ENRICO: Then you do think I have something.

BUONARROTI: Yes.

(There obviously is something else on his mind. ENRICO senses it.)

ENRICO: What.

BUONARROTI: Don't go to Florence. Don't study painting.

ENRICO: Why not?

BUONARROTI: It would be selfish. Your father needs you.

ENRICO: If I were a successful artist I could support my father. He'd never have to work again.

BUONARROTI: But you might fail. Most artists fail, you know. Even some of the bad ones. Better to stay at home and make wine.

(ENRICO lets this sink in for a moment. It's depressing, not the answer he wanted. For lack of anything to say, he offers BUONARROTI more wine.)

ENRICO: Did you want some more?

BUONARROTI: I've had enough, actually.

ENRICO: You don't like it?

BUONARROTI: It's all right.

ENRICO: That's what you said about my drawing.

(BUONARROTI *shrugs.*)

ENRICO: Maybe you just don't like good wine.

BUONARROTI: I know good wine, believe me. This isn't. It's heavy and bitter.

ENRICO: You don't know what you're talking about.

BUONARROTI: I know how something tastes.

ENRICO: You may be a real artist, but I'm a winemaker. We have the finest wine in the region on this farm. We're small, we're not famous. But the wine is good.

BUONARROTI: Have it your way. I say it's heavy and bitter.

ENRICO: I don't know why you have to be so unfriendly.

BUONARROTI: I don't know why you have to be so beautiful.

ENRICO: ... excuse me?

BUONARROTI: You heard me.

ENRICO: I don't know what to say...

BUONARROTI: You could start by telling me why.

ENRICO: I don't know what you mean...

BUONARROTI: Why are you beautiful? It's simple enough, isn't it? You answer my question, I'll answer yours.

ENRICO: First of all, I don't happen to think I'm so....

BUONARROTI: Answer.

ENRICO: However I look, I look that way because...because that's who I am. Because that's how God made me. I had nothing to do with it.

BUONARROTI: Good, very good.

ENRICO: Now you.

BUONARROTI: Why am I so unfriendly? Isn't it obvious? The same reason. Because God made me this way. (*He takes a drink of wine.*) Don't look so dejected. Your wine just isn't for me. What could be simpler.

(ENRICO *gets up and puts the wine back on the low cabinet.*)

ENRICO: You don't have to bother taking it back.

BUONARROTI: I'm not taking it back. I'm explaining. I told you the truth and you didn't want to hear it. That's my business, after all—telling the truth. You probably never thought of it that way, but what I do isn't about chipping away at blocks of marble and dabbing paint onto plaster. It's about telling the truth. It's about going through the door, seeing what's really there, and coming back to tell about it. Not being afraid to tell about it. Everything else is the technique that gets you there. I've gotten very good at it. And once you get good at something it's hard to break the habit. If the truth is unkind, then so be it. Or Amen, as they say in church.

ENRICO: Do you go to church?

BUONARROTI: I *build* churches.

ENRICO: ...you're a liar, then.

BUONARROTI: I've already built a chapel for the San Lorenzo in Florence. I'm going to build a church for the Pope in Rome if they ever get the old one torn down. In the meantime I'm going to paint the ceiling of the Pope's chapel, which I admit isn't the same as actually constructing the building itself, but believe me—after I get done with that ceiling nobody's going to think of that chapel as a building. They're going to think of it as a ceiling and nothing more.

(ENRICO *has finally really gotten furious listening to this.*)

ENRICO: Are you done? Because what I meant was: you're a liar about the way you act. God had nothing to do with it. You like being that way. To me, in particular. I could see it the minute you walked in.

BUONARROTI: You saw that.

ENRICO: Yes.

BUONARROTI: You must be very observant to see all that with one look.

ENRICO: Because I can see things! Because I have an eye—just like an artist.

BUONARROTI: Oh, this again.

ENRICO: What is it, jealousy? Are you so afraid that I might really be good? Is that it?

BUONARROTI: Now you're flattering yourself.

ENRICO: But when you first looked at this—the first thing you said was that I could draw! That it was good!

BUONARROTI: I said it wasn't bad.

ENRICO: That I have to practice. But everyone has to practice! Everyone has something to learn! Even you weren't born the way you are! And for someone who grew up on a farm, this isn't bad. Where would you be now if you had grown up on some mountainside? I could learn. Anyone could learn what they need to be an artist—if they want to badly enough.

BUONARROTI: If that were true, then my donkey could write poetry and the Pope would paint his own ceiling.

ENRICO: I'm an artist! I know I am!

BUONARROTI: If you're so sure, then why do you keep yelling about it?

ENRICO: Because you are Buonarroti!

BUONARROTI: And what is that? What is Buonarroti? It's nothing! I'm nothing! You're nothing! The work—that's the only thing! I can't tell you anything other than that!

ENRICO: I think you're the cruelest man I ever met.

BUONARROTI: And I think that sometimes, underneath cruelty, there is something beautiful. And sometimes, inside of beauty, there can be a thing that's very cruel. *(Pause)* And now I'd like a glass of water. I understand the water up here in the hills is quite good.

(A noise from within. The others are returning from the cellar.)

ENRICO: *(Suddenly, without warning)* Take me with you.

BUONARROTI: What?

ENRICO: I don't care if I have talent. I want to study art. I want to study with you.

BUONARROTI: Pour me the water.

(ENRICO hesitates.)

BUONARROTI: *Pour.*

(ENRICO pours him a glass from a pitcher.)

(GIOVANNI and GIULIANO enter from the cellar, talking as they enter. GIOVANNI, loud and flushed with excitement, goes to the table and blows out the candle.)

GIOVANNI: No, really—completely by accident. Enrico was digging the new well just as I asked him, which was pretty unusual in itself now that I think of it, when all of a sudden he's all stooped over, digging away at something in the dirt. The minute I saw it, I could tell we had something special here.

BUONARROTI: *(To GIULIANO)* And is it? Special?

GIULIANO: It's special, all right. It's very special. Just the way Pliny describes it.

BUONARROTI: And the...condition?

GIULIANO: Intact. Completely intact.

(Overcome, BUONARROTI *puts his face into his hands.* ENRICO *makes a move towards him.)*

ENRICO: Are you all right?

BUONARROTI: I'm fine. Don't touch me. I'm all right.

GIOVANNI: *(To* ENRICO*)* Get the man some wine.

BUONARROTI: I don't want any wine.

GIOVANNI: It's very good wine. We make it our—

BUONARROTI: I don't want the wine!

GIOVANNI: I'm sorry. I thought I'd offer.

*(*BUONARROTI *gets up.)*

BUONARROTI: I want to see it now. I'm ready.

GIOVANNI: Enrico, you go with him.

BUONARROTI: No, I'll go alone.

GIOVANNI: Enrico...

(He gestures for ENRICO *to follow.)*

ENRICO: Here, I'll show you the way.

BUONARROTI: I'd prefer to go alone.

*(*ENRICO *takes him by the arm.)*

ENRICO: It's very dark in the cellar. You can hit your head...

BUONARROTI: Get your hand off me!

GIOVANNI: Mr. Buonarroti, the statue is still mine and I want you accompanied. I'm not asking. Understand?

*(*BUONARROTI *looks at* ENRICO, *then back at* GIOVANNI. *Then to* ENRICO...*)*

BUONARROTI: After you.

*(*ENRICO *lights the candle, goes to the cellar door and goes inside, followed by* BUONARROTI.*)*

GIOVANNI: Some wine?

GIULIANO: I believe I will, thank you.

*(*GIOVANNI *goes to the low cabinet, brings back the wine and two cups. He will pour them out. He talks through all this.)*

GIOVANNI: Quite a charmer, that Buonarroti.

GIULIANO: You must forgive him. He's a decent man, really, but very...unhappy.

GIOVANNI: Yes, must be tough. All those dinners with the Pope.

GIULIANO: He doesn't care about that sort of thing.

GIOVANNI: Then we're the same that way. Neither do I.

GIULIANO: *(Confidentially)* He enjoys men.

GIOVANNI: Yes...?

GIULIANO: You understand what I mean? Instead of women.

GIOVANNI: You think I never heard of that? I live on a mountain, not the moon.

GIULIANO: Well, it's against church teaching.

GIOVANNI: So is the church.

GIULIANO: Excuse me...?

GIOVANNI: Against church teaching.

GIULIANO: I'd be careful, saying things like that. They have ways of finding out, you know. People get burned for less than that.

GIOVANNI: Oh they already know about me. But they'd have to come all the way up this mountain to get me. Apparently I'm not worth it.

GIULIANO: They sent someone for this statue, didn't they?

GIOVANNI: But the statue is important.

(He smiles and hands GIULIANO *a cup of wine.)*

GIULIANO: Perhaps we should discuss the...particulars.

GIOVANNI: You mean, a price.

GIULIANO: Did you...have a figure in mind?

GIOVANNI: Well, I've been thinking. I'm not so sure I want to sell.

GIULIANO: You...what?

GIOVANNI: I just don't know.

GIULIANO: Well, I—I don't understand, I....

GIOVANNI: What would I do with all that money?

GIULIANO: Forget the money—what would you do with a statue?

GIOVANNI: Well, it's something to look at. It's nice to have pretty things to look at.

GIULIANO: Yes, but with the money, you go down into the village and hire a couple of men and get them to come up here to tend your vines for you. Then you sit in your house, a few servants to wait on you, and you enjoy the rest of your life. That's not so bad, is it?

GIOVANNI: Well, but all the same...

GIULIANO: All the same—what?

GIOVANNI: There's my son.

GIULIANO: What about him?

GIOVANNI: He wants to go with you.

GIULIANO: With me?

GIOVANNI: With this Buonarroti fellow. He wants to study art. But he's guilty about leaving the old man on the mountaintop. He thinks he's fooling me. He lies. "No, papa. I don't want to be an artist. I don't want to be a painter." But I know. I can see it. The more he denies it, the more I know.

GIULIANO: And you won't let him go?

GIOVANNI: But he's not very good. That's the real problem.

GIULIANO: So you're not going to sell.

GIOVANNI: How can I? Better to keep the statue, forget about the money, and keep my son where he belongs. Everyone is better off.

GIULIANO: *(Grasping at straws...)* ...don't you think that's a little—selfish?

GIOVANNI: Selfish? I'm doing him a favor.

GIULIANO: You can't keep him here where he doesn't want to be.

GIOVANNI: Why not?

GIULIANO: It's not Christian.

GIOVANNI: That's right, I forgot—you're the expert. It's not me keeping him, don't you see? It's God. Enrico prayed and asked for the gift and God said no. God does that once in a while. Have you noticed? It's God who's keeping him here, or Fate, whatever you want to call it. Like the snakes on those men in the statue. It's Fate that's dragging him down and there's nothing to do about it. All I'm doing is accepting it.

(He takes a deep, well-satisfied drink of wine. A slight pause. GIULIANO *swallows hard. Then slowly, painfully...)*

GIULIANO: I'm willing to go high as three thousand.

(Pause)

GIOVANNI: Lump sum?

GIULIANO: Yes.

(Pause)

GIOVANNI: I'll settle for two thousand. Plus an annuity of two hundred fifty.

GIULIANO: For the rest of your life...

GIOVANNI: For the rest of his life.

GIULIANO: My God...!

GIOVANNI: *(Shrugging)* Take it or leave it. It's up to you.

GIULIANO: I'm not sure that I'm authorized!

GIOVANNI: Like I said, I wouldn't mind keeping the statue. Might be for the best.

GIULIANO: I, uh...I'm a little hungry. And the wine is—uh... *(He gestures to his head.)* ...I wonder if you might have some food, give me a chance to think about this for a moment.

(GIOVANNI smiles warmly.)

GIOVANNI: Absolutely. Come upstairs. We'll have dinner while we wait.

(GIOVANNI goes to the outside door. GIULIANO starts to follow.)

GIOVANNI: You can meet my daughter Liccia. You'll like Liccia. She's very pretty, and she's not married yet. Tell me, are you married yourself?

GIULIANO: No, my wife died a few years ag—

GIOVANNI: Because Liccia is very hard working. All day scrubbing and cooking and what a cook she is. Wait 'til you taste her...

(They are gone.)

(The door to the cellar slams open. BUONARROTI appears seeming slightly dazed, unsure where to move. ENRICO appears at the door behind him. He blows out the candle. He talks nervously.)

ENRICO: I knew you'd feel this way about it. I did too, the moment I saw it, I did too. Papa doesn't appreciate these things, but I—I know something great when I see it. *(Going towards him...)* That's what I want to do. I want to be an artist like that, I want to be able to—!

BUONARROTI: *(Cutting him off)* For God's sake, just shut up, would you?! *(Pause)* You don't understand, do you.

When God made the world, he...*created*—something. In the truest sense, the real sense of the word: to bring into being. There is nothing, now there is something. That's what God did. We forget that—there was nothing. *Nothing.* And now...the world. The stars, the sun...
(He runs his fingers along the table top and looks at his fingertips.)
...dust, air, stones. You. I.

When an artist paints, or a sculptor hammers the stone—that's not creation. We're just...rearranging things. It looks new, it seems as if we've created something, but no—forget it. It's not possible. Only God creates things and he's long since finished.

But...sometimes, once in a thousand years, there is a work of man that *seems* to be new. That seems to be actually created. The material seems not

to have been there before, and now it is.
(He gestures behind him, to the inner door.)
That...that creation in your cellar is one of these.

   Laocoon, he's the man, the father, a Trojan priest. He reaches up to escape the serpent's grasp and...
(Unconsciously, he begins to imitate the figures in the statue.)
...his head rears back just at the moment of knowledge, the moment of despair, knowing that the reach is futile. He knows in this instant that he will die in the serpent's terrible grip. And his sons will die too. That all is lost. Yet the moment is about the *struggle*, the agonizing struggle that must go on! Now, and forever. *Now, this precise moment! And forever!*

   If ever man came close to God, it was in that piece of stone in your cellar. In that marble, man has created something which comes breathlessly close, heart-stoppingly close to God's own creation.

   And you casually stroll out the door and say you'd like to do that too. Well, you can't! It doesn't happen that way! Nobody can! Even *I* can't!

ENRICO: I'm sorry, I...that's not what I—I only meant I was inspired, I want to do great things.

BUONARROTI: It's fake, that kind of inspiration. You don't get inspiration from art, you get it from life. Good art only intimidates you into doing it a little better.

ENRICO: I'm sorry.

BUONARROTI: You might as well learn it now. You will never, never create such a thing as that!

ENRICO: All right! I hear you!

BUONARROTI: Yes, but do you understand me?

ENRICO: Yes.

BUONARROTI: Then that's the end of it! No more talk of going to Florence!

(ENRICO picks up the bottle of wine and carries it back to a side cabinet. He pours himself a cup and drinks it before returning it to the shelf.)

ENRICO: I'm sorry if I upset you.

BUONARROTI: You didn't.

ENRICO: Well, anyway—I apologize.

BUONARROTI: You had to know, that's all. No one around here is able to tell you. But I could and I did. The truth, remember?

ENRICO: I meant that maybe I upset you because I reminded you of your own shortcomings.

BUONARROTI: Mine?

ENRICO: Isn't that really why you're angry? Because I reminded you that even you won't ever make anything like the statue?

(BUONARROTI *starts to smile...*)

ENRICO: Laugh if you want. You weren't just a second ago. I guess we all have our limitations. I have mine, but you have yours. You told me why I'll never be an artist. But you said something about yourself at the same time, and when you heard it come out—you didn't like it much.

BUONARROTI: Wrong!
  The reason you'll never be an artist? Not because I say so. Because you listened to me when I said it! Because you didn't laugh in my face and say "The hell with you, Buonarroti! What do you know?!" You'll defend your wine to the death, but your passion for art? I talked you out of it in two minutes.

ENRICO: But even you can't do what that sculptor has done! You said so yourself!

BUONARROTI: No...that's right: I can't. (*He leans forward with enormous conviction.*) I can do better. I'll take what he's done and I'll go farther, I'll be greater, I'll do more. That's why I'm an artist, because I believe that I can. I might be wrong, but I believe. It's all the difference.

(*The outside door opens and* GIOVANNI *enters followed by* GIULIANO *chewing on a piece of bread.*)

GIULIANO: Oh, you're back! Good!

GIOVANNI: We went upstairs for a little something to eat but your lazy sister forgot to make dinner.

GIULIANO: Well? Did you see?

BUONARROTI: Yes.

GIULIANO: Good, because we came to an agreement, financially speaking.

(GIOVANNI *looks to* ENRICO.)

GIOVANNI: I think you'll be happy with the amount.

GIULIANO: Two thousand, plus a...small annuity.

GIOVANNI: What did we say? I forgot.

GIULIANO: Three hundred. (*Aside, to* BUONARROTI) You don't think it's too much, do you?

BUONARROTI: The sculpture is beyond price.

GIULIANO: Right, that's what I thought.

BUONARROTI: We're lucky he doesn't want to keep it for himself.

GIULIANO: Well, good then. Should we go?

BUONARROTI: Everything is done?

GIULIANO: We've signed an agreement. I'll be back out tomorrow with some workmen and a carriage. *(Pointedly, to* GIOVANNI.*)* And the money. Nothing to do tonight, but go home and get some sleep.

GIOVANNI: It's not raining so hard. And the wind is stopped.

GIULIANO: Yes, well, there we are. See you tomorrow. We'll be here by noon.

*(*BUONARROTI *stands.)*

BUONARROTI: Thank you for your hospitality. I apologize if I was abrupt, earlier. I was nervous about seeing it.

GIOVANNI: Well it's all worked out fine, hasn't it.

BUONARROTI: Yes, I think it has. *(He goes back to* ENRICO.*)* Do you ever come to Rome?

ENRICO: Why?

BUONARROTI: I thought you might come see my chapel ceiling when it's finished. I already have ideas for it. It's going to be very beautiful. Not as beautiful as you, but after all you will always be the original, made by God. *(He goes to the outside door.)* Come.

(He exits followed by GIULIANO.*)*

*(*GIOVANNI *closes the door after them. A slight beat)*

GIOVANNI: Did he try something with you?

ENRICO: Oh Papa, for God's sake...

GIOVANNI: Listen, you bring your goods to market, sometimes you have to throw in a little something extra to close the deal.

ENRICO: He was here for the statue. That's all he cared about.

GIOVANNI: I made the deal without you.

ENRICO: It doesn't matter.

GIOVANNI: Well I'm sorry. I said I'd wait for you.

ENRICO: You did not. You told me to mind my own business.

GIOVANNI: Enrico, how can you get things wrong so much? I wonder about you. I promised I'd consult you before I closed the deal. And I didn't—but for two thousand plus the annuity! How could I hesitate? I promised to throw in a case of our best wine, to be drunk by the Pope himself.

ENRICO: I thought you couldn't care less about the Pope.

GIOVANNI: He drinks a lot of wine. I could learn to care about him.

ENRICO: You have your money, that's the important thing.

GIOVANNI: It'll be yours soon.

ENRICO: Not so soon, I don't think.

GIOVANNI: I could die anytime.

ENRICO: You've said that for years.

GIOVANNI: It's been true for years.

ENRICO: Go to bed, Papa.

(GIOVANNI *stays where he is.*)

GIOVANNI: I got everything I wanted, and then some. Don't you want to know what I plan on doing with it?

ENRICO: What, Papa?

GIOVANNI: It's enough to send you to Florence. You could study.

(ENRICO *doesn't know how to answer.*)

GIOVANNI: I know it's what you want.

(*Pause*)

ENRICO: I don't think so.

GIOVANNI: What do you mean? Why not?

ENRICO: A few years ago, maybe. Not anymore.

GIOVANNI: What are you talking about? You're twenty two years old. People learn to draw when they're twenty two. Besides, you already know how. You only need to get better.

ENRICO: When I was younger, I think maybe then I might have become an artist. But...you change, Papa. A person changes. Then it's not possible anymore.

GIOVANNI: That's a bunch of crap! What are you talking about?

ENRICO: When the grape is ready to be picked, you pick it. If you wait, the grape is no good, not for wine. Good for other things, maybe. Not for wine. Not for a great wine. There's nothing anyone can do to change that. And you know it, Papa.

GIOVANNI: You're not a grape.

ENRICO: I'm not an artist.

GIOVANNI: (*Shrugs*) Well, have it your way.

ENRICO: Thank you, Papa.

(GIOVANNI *starts to leave.*)

ENRICO: I do know when to pick the grape, though, don't I.

GIOVANNI: Like no one I ever saw. You have the knack.

ENRICO: It's honorable, wine-making. Isn't it.

GIOVANNI: I always thought so.

ENRICO: So did I. Good night Papa.

GIOVANNI: Good night.

(GIOVANNI *goes out and closes the door.*)

(ENRICO *goes to cabinet, gets the bottle of wine and a cup, and sits at the table. He pours a little in the cup and drinks.*)

(*Then he arranges the grapes in the bowl, and sets the candle at a better angle to it. He produces the sketching paper and a piece of charcoal from his pocket.*)

(*He presses the paper flat onto the table, eyes the fruit bowl, and begins to sketch the still life scene in front of him.*)

(*The lights fade to black.*)

END OF PART TWO

Part Three
LEVELS OF PERCEPTION

(The late 1980s)

*(The terrace of a house in the East End of Long Island—"the Hamptons."
A door upstage leading into the house. S L exit goes towards a barn, now
serving as an artist's studio. S R exit goes towards the driveway.)*

(11 A M. Summer. A beautiful, sun-drenched day)

(Several chairs and a table are set out on the terrace.)

*(SALLY, forties, sits in one of the chairs, reading a magazine, sipping at a cup
of coffee.)*

*(GENE, sixties, enters from stage left. He carries a basket of tomatoes. He goes to
look around the corner to the driveway.)*

SALLY: He's not here yet.

GENE: No, I was just uh....

SALLY: Enjoying the view?

GENE: Yes.

SALLY: Pretty driveway, isn't it. Gravel's a nice touch. *(She looks back to her
magazine.)*

GENE: I don't want him getting the jump on me.

SALLY: Three-hour drive this time of year. Traffic and all. I say one o'clock
at the earliest.

(Pause)

GENE: How long is he staying?

SALLY: He didn't say.

GENE: You didn't ask him?

SALLY: Don't worry. You know he won't want to spend a night outside the
city. He's like a vampire—always home by sunset.

GENE: A vampire would be sunrise I think.

SALLY: You get the idea.

(Beat. SALLY reads. GENE examines the tomatoes.)

GENE: Good tomatoes this year.

SALLY: They're wonderful.

GENE: Eat 'em like apples.

SALLY: Mmm.

GENE: What are you going to tell him?

SALLY: What am I going to...?—*I'm* not saying anything. This is your business.

GENE: But you're so much better at this—

SALLY: There's nothing to be good at.

GENE: Please? I'll get scarce, you tell him, he'll go away, I'll make tomato soup.

SALLY: If you want me to tell him to go away, that I can do. But if anyone is going to give him the news, Gene, that person is you.

GENE: I thought that's what I had you for.

(The sound of a car pulling in)

GENE: Oh God.

SALLY: If you explain, he'll understand.

(GENE looks around him.)

GENE: No he won't. I've got to hide.

SALLY: Don't you dare. He's come all the way from the city.

(Car doors open and slam shut. He pecks her on the forehead.)

GENE: Thank you. You've never let me down.

(He exits the way he came, towards the studio. She looks after him, annoyed. She makes a decision, then exits into the house.)

(A young man, ALAN, enters. He stops as though sensing something strange.)

ALAN: Damn. It's got a *vibe.*

(LEONARD appears behind him.)

LEONARD: What did you say?

ALAN: This place, it's got his vibe. I can feel him.

(He has sunk to his knees, putting his cheek on the earth. LEONARD rolls his eyes.)

LEONARD: Alan, this is me. You can save the drama.

(ALAN stands up satisfied—not in response to LEONARD.)

ALAN: You could feel it too if you weren't so fucking tense. Where do you think he is?

LEONARD: Hiding.

ALAN: Hiding?

LEONARD: Gene likes to hide. It's why he left the city, came here. It was remote at the time. Hard to get to. Suited him perfectly.

(ALAN *wanders around, inspecting the details of the place.*)

ALAN: Well, it's a good pose, anyway.

LEONARD: It's not a pose. Gene's not the posing type.

ALAN: You don't take a place in The Hamptons if it's not some kind of pose.

LEONARD: It wasn't 'The Hamptons' at the time, it was the East End: potato farmers and fishermen. It was cheap, and the light was good, and nobody bothered him. That's why they all came—Pollock, de Kooning. All of them. Gene's not a poseur. He's no good at it.

ALAN: That's what makes him good at it: that he's not 'good at it'.

LEONARD: Your problem is you have no perspective.

ALAN: (*Stung, angry...*) No Leonard, it's not lack of perspective. It's a different one. My perspective is that I understand perception and the perception is Gene Kaap lives in the Hamptons. That's what people say. That's how they think of it. They don't think about old potato farms. They think Gene Kaap/Hamptons, Hamptons/Gene Kaap. One does not see him moving to some other potato farm in some other remote area, does one. A pose is a pose, whether it's stumbled upon by accident or deliberately struck. He's associating himself with the place. It's all about marketing, Leonard, raising the value of the work. A subject you'd know something about.

LEONARD: Gene's got all the money he can use.

ALAN: A man with a lot of money and a major reputation goes to some effort to acquire greater cachet and make even more money. Why. Because he can, Leonard. Back to Art Dealer School with you.

(LEONARD *stands.*)

LEONARD: I shouldn't have brought you.

ALAN: I'm only telling the truth and you know it.

LEONARD: If you embarrass me in front of him...

ALAN: Oh Leonard, relax. Gene and I are going to get along fine.

LEONARD: Just don't screw it up. This is too important. I'm going to look for him. (*He goes to exit to the orchard.*)

ALAN: Shouldn't you try the house? *(He points to the house.)*

LEONARD: He's not there.

ALAN: How do you know?

LEONARD: There's one thing you should know about me: I know Gene. *(He leaves.)*

*(*ALAN *watches him go, then drops down to put his face to the ground again.)*

*(*SALLY *appears at the screen door, and, not seeing* ALAN, *she enters. He looks up, she sees him, but it's too late. They look at each other.)*

ALAN: You must be Mrs Kaap.

SALLY: And you are?

ALAN: Alan.

SALLY: *(Lightly, not snide)* What, is that like Cher? You're "Alan"?

ALAN: Alan Becker.

SALLY: *(A light goes off)* Wait a second... *(She picks up the magazine.)* ...I was just—aren't you in here?

ALAN: *(Looking at the cover)* Oh, this is old.

SALLY: *(Looking for the article)* Well, we're a little behind the times around here. Here you are. "Installation Nation: Alan Becker and the Art of Perception."

ALAN: I wasn't that happy with it, actually.

SALLY: No?

ALAN: Not the magazine piece, that was fine. I meant my installation— it never really seemed to work totally.

SALLY: You're being modest.

ALAN: No, it's true. It was too direct, too—I don't know....

SALLY: *(Encouraging him to go on...)* Yes?

ALAN: Too...*clear.*

SALLY: Right.

ALAN: My work has to be more veiled, more stratified. It's got to... you can't take it head on. It has to be....

SALLY: ...less clear.

ALAN: Right.

SALLY: Less emotional.

ALAN: Well, not without some kind of...*slant* anyway.

SALLY: Got it.

ALAN: I'm doing this new installation downtown at Kinesis—you know it?

SALLY: *(Not completely sure)* Kinesis...

ALAN: It's new. Anyway, my piece is going to be good, I think. I hope. I mean, if things work out...

(He wants to say something but can't. She's aware of that and chooses to move on regardless.)

SALLY: Where's Leonard?

ALAN: He went to look for Gene.

SALLY: In the studio?

ALAN: *(Looking off stage...)* If that's the studio back there. Leonard seemed to think he was hiding.

SALLY: Oh did he.

ALAN: Is he?

SALLY: Oh, I don't speak for Gene. That's a long-standing policy. I'm not about to break it. Hungry?

ALAN: Uh...no. Thanks.

SALLY: I hope you like tomatoes. Bumper crop this year. We're having them for lunch.

ALAN: ...could I ask you something?

(She looks at him, non-committal.)

ALAN:Do you think it would be okay if I kind of...talked to him? Alone?

SALLY: To Gene?

ALAN: Yeah.

SALLY: About what?

ALAN: Well—his work, basically. The old stuff—from the fifties and sixties.

SALLY: I'm afraid they were all bought a very long time ago—

ALAN: *Buy* one!? What do you think I am? A millionaire? Jesus, no. I just want to...I'd just love to *talk* to him about them.

SALLY: Oh, well, he loves to talk....

ALAN: I mean, not *just* talk. It's about this new project. I got an idea on the way out here, in the car. I really think it might be kind of genius.

SALLY: What kind of idea?

ALAN: I can't tell you.

SALLY: Why not?

ALAN: It wouldn't be right. It wouldn't come out the right way.

SALLY: How would it come out?

ALAN: Look, I know you're the gatekeeper...

SALLY: I beg your pardon.

ALAN: Mrs Kaap, I don't want to dance around. That's what you are, everybody knows that.

SALLY: Well I hate to be the one to—

ALAN: Which I respect. That's why I'm coming to you directly, for permission. Just to talk to him.

SALLY: And you can't say what it's about.

ALAN: It's not about sales or contracts or money. That much I guarantee. I guess I just want his blessing for what I want to do.

SALLY: I'm sorry, but this is all just too vague...

ALAN: Okay, look. What I do in my work—it's about perception. Getting people to look on different levels. When Gene was starting out, all he had to do was paint.

SALLY: Actually he had to paint *well*....

ALAN: Of course...

SALLY: That part was always crucial....

ALAN: Yes, of course...

SALLY: But often forgotten...

ALAN: I didn't mean that. Of course. You're right. But that's still my point—you could simply be very good. Which is hard enough—but at least there wasn't this whole other level of having to make some sort of splash that has nothing to do with being "very good."

SALLY: I don't see why you're complaining.

ALAN: It's not a complaint—

SALLY: That article seems to say that making a splash is your *forte*.

ALAN: It's an observation. I don't complain.

SALLY: And this idea of yours, the reason you want to talk to Gene— it's about making that splash.

ALAN: It has artistic merit.

(She only stares at him.)

ALAN: This isn't going to do it justice, because you have to be there and see it to understand. I mean, it would be like explaining one of Gene Kaap's paintings to someone who's never seen one.

SALLY: Try me.

ALAN: *(Suddenly into it)* Okay, I converted the entire floor of the gallery into a blacktop, like the surface of an old parking lot. Worked into the floor, I have coins, I have matches, I have cigarettes, bottle tops, pop tops, rubber bands, paper clips, condoms, nuts, bolts, screws, old wire, audio tape, gum, candy wrappers. The detritus of a so-called civilization.

So you walk into this gallery and the first thing you notice is that you don't really notice anything. Because there's nothing on the walls. It's all on the floor, and the entire floor is the installation, so you don't see it right away—you don't *recognize* it. You just think—"oh, this building has a really weird floor." And it's Soho, so you figure, this was a garage or something, and nobody ever bothered to fix up the floor.

So you go into the back, where there's an office, and you ask where the installation is, and they say 'out front.' And you go back out front and you look again, and then—maybe, if you're smart—you look down and you think "Wait a minute. This is it. This is the installation." Which is when you start to get it.

The exciting moment is when they begin to see, to apprehend the true nature of what they're looking at—the moment of the shift, the revelation of meaning. They're forced to stop looking at it one way, and start looking at it another. That's what it's all about. And the problem is, that's not happening. I have to incorporate another level of apprehension.

SALLY: Which is where Gene comes in...

ALAN: Exactly.

SALLY: How?

ALAN: That's what I can't tell you. I've got to say it to him. It wouldn't feel right otherwise.

SALLY: I'm afraid I haven't seen him all morning.

ALAN: But he's around...

SALLY: Sometimes he's gone for hours...

ALAN: He should be the one to decide—you said so yourself. Otherwise it's really you who's making the decision...

(LEONARD has entered during this. SALLY sees him before ALAN does and uses it as an escape.)

SALLY: Leonard...

(She rises, they kiss.)

LEONARD: You're looking very well.

SALLY: Spoken like an expert in press relations.

LEONARD: Whatever he wants, don't trust him.

ALAN: Oh that's nice.

LEONARD: Or at least make him pay for it.

ALAN: This is my own dealer talking.

SALLY: *(To* LEONARD*)* You didn't find him out there?

LEONARD: No.

SALLY: Well, he does disappear, you know.

LEONARD: You don't know where he is?

ALAN: She doesn't give up much info, Leonard.

SALLY: You know Gene. In the old days he might be gone for *days.*

LEONARD: Yes, but that was the old days.

SALLY: Some things never change.

LEONARD: *(Tiring of this...)* Sally, where is he?

SALLY: I don't have the foggiest.

(Slight pause)

LEONARD: Alan, there's lots of weird rusted iron...*stuff* behind the barn. Why don't you go have a look.

ALAN: Leonard, I'm a big boy now...

LEONARD: If you find something you want, maybe Sally will let you throw it in the trunk.

ALAN: You're so subtle. *(He exits.)*

SALLY: We're not going to have a scene now, are we?

LEONARD: I hope not.

SALLY: How about a tomato? They're really good. We grow them out by the studio. Gene's very proud of them.

LEONARD: Sally, stop it.

SALLY: I tried to tell you about his health.

LEONARD: You said he got tired.

SALLY: Yes. He's probably tired.

LEONARD: Then he's inside, lying down.

SALLY: No, he's—he might have gone for a walk.

LEONARD: Well which is it?

SALLY: I don't know.

LEONARD: Sally...

SALLY: I tried to warn you on the phone—

LEONARD: ...if you're interfering somehow—

SALLY: —but he was standing there in the room. I couldn't very well spell it all out.

LEONARD: Spell what out?

SALLY: His mind, Leonard. *(Pause. She struggles....)* It's...well, it's not *gone*, not completely. He'll be right here, perfectly fine. I'll go inside the house to answer the phone, come back out and...he'll be gone. Here, but disappeared into some...blank, empty place.
    And sometimes...he's *gone* gone. He went out to the studio one morning and never came back. I finally had to call the police. He'd gotten lost a hundred yards from the house—ended up in Water Mill. Didn't recognize a thing. Two days later, he woke up the same old Gene again.

LEONARD: *(Stunned...)* How long has this been going on?

SALLY: He started to forget things after we moved out here full time. For five years he worked everyday, though. And even after that he still went out to the studio because—well, he always said that painting was like going through a secret door, into another world. And who would stop trying to go through that door—even if he couldn't find it?

LEONARD: God, Sally...I'm sorry.

SALLY: Oh, I'm used to it now. The only hard part is—he'll be gone for good one day. That I won't like.

LEONARD: I always thought you were the one good thing he ever had.

SALLY: Well, I wouldn't go that far...

LEONARD: Face it, except for you—who was there?

SALLY: *(Smiling ruefully)* Well, no one else was crazy enough to be in love with him. Then again, I had his work. I always had the feeling Gene was speaking right to me, saying all the things he couldn't say otherwise. *(Her smile evaporates.)* Oh Jesus, I've got to stop that.

LEONARD: But it's true...

SALLY: No—talking in the past tense. There'll be plenty of time for that.

LEONARD: You were the only one who never wanted anything of him. That includes me. And nothing much has changed, I'm afraid. *(Pause)* I'm broke.

(She looks at him as if she didn't hear correctly.)

LEONARD: Out of money.

SALLY: That's impossible.

LEONARD: I used to think so too.

SALLY: You've got a gallery full of work.... *(Referring to the magazine again)* I keep reading about it.

LEONARD: Oh, the work is still there. A year ago it was worth three and a half, maybe four million. Today...well, today I wish there were a market for scrap canvas.

It's over, Sally. Nobody's had that kind of money since the crash—and what they've got they aren't spending on art. I'm stuck.

SALLY: *(With a nod out towards the studio) Enfant terrible* can't help you out?

LEONARD: Are you kidding?

SALLY: He seems to be all the rage.

LEONARD: Yeah, but it's tough to take an asphalt floor containing 'the detritus of our so-called civilization' and hang it over your couch.
   I know about the paintings, Sally.

SALLY: What paintings?

LEONARD: Stop it. I got a call from Misha Kansky and he said Gene had mentioned them.

SALLY: I knew it.

LEONARD: Sally, these are important paintings. From what you're saying, maybe the last he'll ever do. The world deserves to see them. Gene deserves to show them.

SALLY: Leonard, I can't.

LEONARD: And you know I'm the person to sell them.

SALLY: You would be, of course, if—

LEONARD: I'd do it right. Tasteful, but profitable.

SALLY: You just said you couldn't sell anything.

LEONARD: *(Surprised she needs this explanation...)* New work by Gene Kaap... that I can sell. It's been fifteen years. Do you know how badly people want to see what he's done in that time? It's one of the great mysteries of the art world—what has Gene Kaap been up to since then.

SALLY: Leonard, it's not up to me. You know that. Gene and I have always agreed that the work is his. His to sell, his to keep, his to do with as he pleases.

LEONARD: *(With difficulty...)* They're going to seize the assets.

SALLY: Your paintings?

LEONARD: Not just the paintings. The gallery. The apartment. My socks and underwear. Everything.

SALLY: Oh my God...

LEONARD: They'd be gone already but I was able to convince them I had a shot at this. Thank God I found a bank officer who had actually heard of him. I kept dropping his name in front of these blank-eyed C P As....

Sally, at least show them to me.

SALLY: I'm sorry. You're going to have to talk to Gene. It's the only way.

LEONARD: Boy are you tough.

SALLY: I'm not tough, Leonard.

LEONARD: You really think you're doing him a favor when you act like this.

SALLY: No, I think I don't have a choice. *(She looks at him, feeling bad.)* Let me show you the garden. The tomatoes really are quite good this year. You want to go pick a basket?

LEONARD: I don't like tomatoes.

SALLY: You don't have to eat them. You can just look at them.

(She heads to the studio. He still hesitates.)

SALLY: Maybe we'll find him out there.

LEONARD: *(He takes the basket.)* Lead the way.

(They exit.)

(After a moment, GENE enters from the house. He looks both ways then goes to retrieve the tomatoes.)

(ALAN enters from the driveway. GENE is caught.)

GENE: Shit.

ALAN: Hi.

GENE: You must be the...uh...in the magazine... *(He nods to the magazine, which happens to be near.)*

ALAN: Alan Becker.

GENE: Right. Gene Kaap.

ALAN: I know.

GENE: Where's Leonard?

ALAN: I don't know. They were just here. Maybe she's showing him your studio.

GENE: Oh yeah?

ALAN: We could stop them.

GENE: No, I don't give a shit.

ALAN: Well, this is an honor.

(He goes to shake GENE's *hand.* GENE *puts down the tomatoes and they shake.)*

ALAN: For the longest time, I thought you were dead.

GENE: Yeah, me too.

ALAN: I hope it's okay I'm here. I happened to run into Leonard last night at an opening and—well, I really had to beg him. Because of your privacy and all.

GENE: Nice of him.

ALAN: It is kind of perfect, though, isn't it.

GENE: Is it?

ALAN: That we got the chance to meet.

GENE: Why is that perfect?

ALAN: Well—one generation to another. Former iconoclast to current iconoclast.

GENE: Oh. Right.

ALAN: Well, you were. I mean, you are.

GENE: That's a lot of bullshit. If I could have been Norman Rockwell, believe me—in a heartbeat.

ALAN: *(Genuine)* You know, I respect the hell out of that.

GENE: You do?

ALAN: You are what you have to be—no complaints. That's exactly why I thought I could— *(He glances out to the studio to make sure they're alone....)* —listen, I've got this idea. Do you mind if I just pitch it to you? It's crazy but...is that okay?

GENE: I don't know. I never got pitched before.

ALAN: I've got a show coming up, an installation at Kinesis. And I had this idea, coming out here in the car, that you—your work, I want to use it.

GENE: I don't do group shows.

ALAN: No, that's not what I—

GENE: I always come off looking bad.

ALAN: Gene, it's not—

GENE: My stuff is fragile—

ALAN: —can I call you Gene—?

GENE: —it doesn't look fragile but it is.

ALAN: It's not a group show. It's an installation. But I want you to be in it—be part of it. Or it to be part of you—whichever way you want to think about it.

(GENE *is completely confused.*)

ALAN: You're not getting this.

GENE: No...

ALAN: What I did was, I converted the floor into a blacktop, like the surface of an old parking lot. Then I worked all of kinds of...*junk* basically—the detritus....

GENE: ...of a so-called civilization.

ALAN: *(How did he know that...?)* Right...

˙GENE: I was listening at the window.

ALAN: *(Barely a pause to regroup)* So you—okay. But what I didn't say is...the idea was—originally—that the walls were bare, so that you came into the gallery and saw bare walls and thought "what's this? Bare walls. Nothing here." And then slowly, *eventually* you caught onto the floor.

But in the car, on the way out here, I got to thinking, "Well here I am, meeting Gene Kaap. That's got to mean something. What does it mean?"

GENE: And what did it mean?

ALAN: What if we took posters—not the actual paintings—but posters of your work from the mid-sixties...you know, *Inversion #5 or Black On Red*—and we hang them on the wall, so they're sort of like *looking down* on this...this *trash* really. This remnant of culture. I mean that just sounds so exciting—and for you, such a great way for people to see your work again. To see it new, fresh.

GENE: Who the fuck *are* you?

ALAN: Look, I'm sort of excited. I'm not explaining it very well. But it's a way to bridge the gap, you see?

GENE: What *gap*?

ALAN: Between you and me, the past and present, your world and this one.

GENE: This is bullshit.

ALAN: Look, what I do...it's different than what you did. You haven't been around.

GENE: Yeah, and I'm starting to feel grateful.

ALAN: This is a tribute. It's an homage.

GENE: I hate tributes.

ALAN: Well, you could use one, frankly. People don't care anymore, Gene. People aren't talking about you.

GENE: I don't want them to talk about *me*.

ALAN: Or the work.

GENE: This year, they're bored. Next year, a retrospective and I'm re-discovered.

ALAN: Yes, exactly.

GENE: For that I don't need your help.

ALAN: I hate to say it but you do.

GENE: Stuck up on a poster? A decoration on the wall?

ALAN: Because it won't just be your work. It'll be a comment on my work.

GENE: Nobody's putting up any posters of anything of mine, anywhere.

ALAN: Well, I don't exactly need your permission. The posters exist.

GENE: Not for that purpose.

ALAN: No. For advertising. And that's okay I suppose. And for sale in the museum shops. And that's okay too. You're happy to stoop when it comes to merchandising. *(He realizes this is only making it worse.)* Look, I admire and respect you. And your work.

GENE: Forgive if I'm not flattered. People see my work everyday, all over the world, and so far they haven't needed you to help them. Go ask Pollock or Newman or Rothko if they want to be in your installation. They're all dead. They can't say no.

ALAN: Oh you can't say no either.

GENE: I just did.

ALAN: Anybody can buy a poster of your work and hang it on a wall and say, "This is a poster of Gene Kaap's *Black On Red*." There's no copyright law against that.

GENE: I'll sue.

ALAN: Good, I could use the publicity. Especially when you lose.

GENE: Listen you pipsqueak. I made something. That makes it mine. You can't have it.

ALAN: Oh, come on. Did you really "make something"? You put paint on canvas, yes. But you were only translating. "Create" is this word some egomaniac came up with to convince himself that what he was doing was important. And art was important. But now, we've done it. We've been there. There is no such thing as creativity. Only arrangement. And I'm not afraid to say it.

GENE: When I painted the world the way I painted the world—nobody had ever done that before. I created the emotions, in here.... *(His torso...)* ...and I created the means by which to express them. That paint and those feelings, together—that was something new.

ALAN: You're really letting this get way too emotional.

GENE: Right! Because you wouldn't know an emotion if it crawled up your ass hole and built a nest there.

(This is stinging—it's enough for ALAN.*)*

ALAN: You know, I'd heard you were arrogant, but....

GENE: You heard right...

ALAN: But a philistine—that I never....

GENE: ...because I draw the line somewhere!

ALAN: *(Lashing out)* Because you can't imagine anyone taking what you did and going the next step. No, the work has to stop with you. You're the pinnacle.

GENE: I never said that.

ALAN: But you don't have to, do you.

GENE: Go further—yes, but the only way you're going is—well, all this relentless *irony*, this intellectualism, the cool surface, the God awful commentary. Where's the humanity?!

ALAN: *(Angry and hurt)* I am responding to the world as it is. As I see it, as I *understand* it. It's different now, Gene. Come down off Mount Olympus... we're struggling down here! You think I wouldn't like it the way it was? You think I'm not jealous of the way you lived and worked? *(Resolved now, sure of himself...)* But that's over. People laugh at emotion now. I laugh at it. And I hate that about the world, but there it is. That's the way it is *now*. What am I supposed to do? Ignore that? I can't make the world a different place, and I can't lie about it either. If it's one thing I won't do, it's lie. Ironic? Yes, guilty—fine. But that's the truth about the world I see. *(Wondering if he went too far)* I love your work, Gene. I honor it. All I'm asking is—let me pay you that honor.

GENE: You're a God damned thief!

(LEONARD and SALLY have entered on this last line. They have a basket of tomatoes.)

LEONARD: You've obviously met.

SALLY: *(Worried...)* Gene...

GENE: Keep your God damned hands off my work!

(He sits down. SALLY goes to him.)

LEONARD: I'm sorry—whatever he said....

ALAN: Hey, I'm not some *criminal.*

LEONARD: We have yet to determine that.

ALAN: I'm allowed to have a point of view.

LEONARD: No you're not.

(LEONARD looks to SALLY, who has gone to GENE.)

SALLY: Are you all right?

GENE: I'm fine.

SALLY: Your breathing is off.

GENE: Oh for Christ's sake I'm all right. Blew the damn carbon out of my pistons, that's all!

SALLY: *(To LEONARD)* He gets like this. I can't do a thing.

LEONARD: What do you mean, 'gets'? He's been like this his whole life, Sally.

GENE: How the hell are you, Len? Get over here.

(LEONARD goes to him. GENE grabs him in a bear hug, then looks at him.)

GENE: You prick. What are you trying to do, bringing this little twit with you? Give me a stroke?

LEONARD: Gene, I'm sorry if he—whatever he said. He's got a mouth....

ALAN: Hey, knock off the apologies...!

SALLY: Gene, you're going to overdo it.

GENE: Good. Let's overdo it. Pipsqueak here got me on a roll.

LEONARD: He's full of himself, okay—but he's also talented.

GENE: Oh gimme a break...

LEONARD: You've never even seen his work.

GENE: I saw that article. *(He indicates the magazine.)*

ALAN: And I suppose you'd want people to judge your work based on a magazine spread.

SALLY: Look, he's had enough for one day...

GENE: You stay out of this.

SALLY: Fine—you boys have your fun. I'm out of it. *(She turns and goes to the house. To ALAN.)* You, with me.

ALAN: You can't talk to me like...

SALLY: Now.

(She opens the door for ALAN, and he has met his match. He lurches angrily into the house. She follows and lets the door slam.)

LEONARD: Gene, I'm sorry—what can I say?

GENE: *(Dismissing it)* You like his stuff. That's your business.

LEONARD: You're angry at me.

GENE: Lennie, it's your business.

LEONARD: He's very good.

GENE: All right—so be it.

LEONARD: It's not what you do. It's environmental. It's experiential. He's got this whole theory about levels of perception and sequential apprehension, and frankly it's pretty God damn brilliant. I think he's going someplace very brave, very daring.

GENE: Sequential appre—!? Jesus! Nobody even speaks the same language anymore. We're all just talking up our own assholes.

LEONARD: But if we don't go there with him, we're cowards. We're safe. Since when is art safe?

GENE: If we go there, the word "art" ceases to have any meaning.

You see? It's impossible. We can't even talk about it. Let's talk about the tomato crop.

LEONARD: Because you're trying to make a comparison.

GENE: I'd just like to know what the kid does.

LEONARD: You've been asking me that for thirty years. You said the same thing about Roy Lichtenstein. "What the hell does that God damn kid do?"

GENE: And I never got an answer *then* either.

LEONARD: But it's beneath you—

GENE: My ass is beneath me—

LEONARD: You don't understand him. Okay. But some people don't understand you either.

GENE: But they understand what I did.

LEONARD: Not everyone—

GENE: If it was any good—and a lot of it wasn't, I'm the first to admit—but if it was any good at all, it was honest to God me. My horror, my wonder. My confusion. My love. It was always me. If it wasn't me, I threw it out.

LEONARD: And there was never anything like it. Before or since.

GENE: You're God damn right.

LEONARD: Which is why I'm here. *(Pause)* I talked to Misha Kansky.

GENE: *(Ready as he'll ever be...)* So?

LEONARD: He was out here. You talked to him. *(A slight beat...)* Gene, I want to see them.

GENE: It's impossible.

LEONARD: I'm in a bad spot here, I—

GENE: I know. I heard. That's my bedroom, right there. *(He indicates the house.)*

LEONARD: I'm the right one for your work. I understand it, I know how to handle it.

(GENE has picked up a tomato and is examining it.)

GENE: Oh yeah, I know that. *(The tomato...)* Beautiful, isn't it. The soil is just right out there behind the barn. You can almost taste the color. If I were a still life kind of guy, I might try to put it on canvas.

LEONARD: Did you?

GENE: *(Smiles ruefully)* I'm not a still life kind of guy.

LEONARD: Gene, I'm asking you. Please. I only want to look at them.

GENE: Oh come on...

LEONARD: It's up to you whether you want to put them on the market. I'm not going to pressure you.
   All right, maybe just a little...

GENE: It wasn't a good time. I wasn't working well.

LEONARD: Why don't you let me be the judge of that?

GENE: Because you're not as sharp as you used to be, frankly.

LEONARD: So you don't trust me—is that it? Because of this kid?

GENE: Lennie, the work was not very good. Period.

LEONARD: And what if you're being too hard on yourself?

GENE: I can't let you see them.

LEONARD: So you're just turning your back on thirty years. On us.

GENE: I can't show you something that doesn't exist.

LEONARD: You had five good years.

GENE: I had five years. Nobody said they were good.

LEONARD: But you must have something!

GENE: I'd have a few good hours, maybe even a day or two at a time. But that's not enough for me. You know the way I work. A day or two? That's nothing! It takes me months—years even.
  Every time I went back to the canvas, it was like starting over. So everything got very simple, very plain, but I kept going. I toughed it out, by God. Trying to draw it out, trying to find the heart of it. And one day I looked back at the work I'd done, and it looked like a child had been playing with my brushes. Scrawls, Lennie. Kid stuff. And I thought, oh god, that's not me. It's some *child*—some person I never was, some *other*. It was the one thing I couldn't live with.
  So we built a bonfire, Sally and I. Out in back of the studio. Built a nice big pyre, lit it and waited until the flames were shooting up, licking at the night sky, and then we took every canvas, forty two of them, and we threw them into the fire, and we watched them turn to vapor. In the morning, nothing but a pile of ashes. Turned out to be good fertilizer. Good for tomatoes. *(He holds up the tomato.)*

LEONARD: All of them?

GENE: It felt so right, Len.

LEONARD: ...they're all gone?

GENE: I didn't know how to tell you. I was chicken shit.

(ALAN enters from the house.)

ALAN: Leonard, listen, I'm going to take the train back.

LEONARD: No, you don't have to—

ALAN: I didn't come out here to peel tomatoes, okay? I can catch the one oh five.

LEONARD: No, we're going. We're done.

(SALLY has entered.)

SALLY: You can't go. I'm making lunch.

LEONARD: I'm sorry.

ALAN: Right now?

LEONARD: Yes.

ALAN: Give me one minute... *(He exits to the studio.)*

SALLY: Now you haven't been *fighting,* have you, because—

GENE: I told him.

SALLY: Oh.

GENE: Len, I disappointed you.

LEONARD: Yes. And also no, in a funny way.

GENE: I did the right thing. I know I did.

(LEONARD goes to him, takes his right hand into his left.)

LEONARD: Yeah.

GENE: You'll get through this with the bank. I'm not worried about you.

LEONARD: Good bye Gene. I can't stay, I hope you understand.

GENE: Drive safe.

(LEONARD crosses towards the driveway. SALLY follows.)

SALLY: *(So that GENE doesn't hear.)* I begged him not to, Len.

LEONARD: You...?

SALLY: I told him, let me save a few. *One,* even. They were gorgeous. Like Matisse at the very end, the way he blossomed into the cut-outs... so simple and so glorious at the same time. That's what these were.

LEONARD: Oh God, don't do this to me...

SALLY: No—it's better you know. They were beautiful...better that than you believing they were nothing at all.

LEONARD: Good bye, Sally.

SALLY: Good bye.

(ALAN enters from the studio with a rusted iron thing. LEONARD exits to the driveway. ALAN takes one furtive shot at GENE.)

ALAN: Think about it. You deserve it.

(GENE stares blankly at him, but ALAN doesn't see that. He hurries away under SALLY's glare.)

(She watches him go. We hear the car start, doors slam. As the car drives away, she turns back to GENE.)

SALLY: Well. Glad that's over.

GENE: *(Questioningly)* I'm sorry....

SALLY: Oh don't worry about it. I knew you'd come through when you had to.

GENE: ...I don't remember your name.

(A slight moment)

SALLY: Sally.

GENE: Sally. Sally Sally Sally.

SALLY: And you're Gene.

GENE: I know.

SALLY: Are you hungry?

GENE: ...yes. Yes, I am.

SALLY: I can make lunch for you. Would you like that?

GENE: Yes.

SALLY: How about a sandwich, with tomatoes?

GENE: Tomatoes?

SALLY: Right here. Tomato.

GENE: Oh...

SALLY: You like tomatoes.

GENE: Yes?

SALLY: Oh yes. You like them very much. Go ahead. Try one.

(She hands him a slice. He bites into it. He likes it.)

GENE: Mmm. That's good.

SALLY: You see? You want me to make a sandwich with tomatoes?

(He nods, his mouth full.)

SALLY: You go ahead and eat the rest of this. There's lots more. We've got a lot of tomatoes. *(She goes to the door.)* Don't go away.

(He nods his head no. She kisses him on the forehead and exits into the house. He eats as the lights go down.)

END OF PLAY

BROADWAY PLAY PUBLISHING INC

ONE ACT COLLECTIONS

THE COLORED MUSEUM

ENSEMBLE STUDIO THEATER MARATHON `84

FACING FORWARD

GIANTS HAVE US IN THEIR BOOKS

ONE ACTS AND MONOLOGUES FOR WOMEN

ORCHARDS

ORGASMO ADULTO ESCAPES FROM THE ZOO

PLAYS BY LOUIS PHILLIPS

ROOTS IN WATER

SHORT PIECES FROM THE NEW DRAMATISTS

WHAT A MAN WEIGHS &
THE WORLD AT ABSOLUTE ZERO

BROADWAY PLAY PUBLISHING INC

PLAYS WITH MORE WOMEN THAN MEN

BESIDE HERSELF

A BRIGHT ROOM CALLED DAY

CHURCH OF THE HOLY GHOST

DAME LORRAINE

A DARING BRIDE

GOONA GOONA

THE LADIES OF FISHER COVE

MINK SONATA

ONLY IN AMERICA

ON THE VERGE

PECONG

PHANTASIE

RAIN. SOME FISH. NO ELEPHANTS.

SHOW AND TELL

STARSTRUCK

STONEWALL JACKSON'S HOUSE

UNFINISHED WOMEN WOMEN CRY IN NO MAN'S LAND
WHILE A BIRD DIES IN A GILDED CAGE

WHAT A MAN WEIGHS

BROADWAY PLAY PUBLISHING INC

PLAYWRIGHTS' COLLECTIONS

PLAYS BY NEAL BELL
MCTEAGUE: A TALE OF SAN FRANCISCO
RAGGED DICK
THÉRÈSE RAQUIN

PLAYS BY ALAN BOWNE
BEIRUT
FORTY-DEUCE
SHARON AND BILLY

PLAYS BY LONNIE CARTER
LEMUEL
GULLIVER
GULLIVER REDUX

PLAYS BY STEVE CARTER
DAME LORRAINE
HOUSE OF SHADOWS
MIRAGE
ONE LAST LOOK
TEA ON INAUGURATION DAY

PLAYS BY ANTHONY CLARVOE
LET'S PLAY TWO
THE LIVING
SHOW AND TELL

PLAYS BY DONALD FREED
ALFRED AND VICTORIA: A LIFE
CHILD OF LUCK
IS HE STILL DEAD?

PLAYS BY ALLAN HAVIS
HOSPITALITY
MINK SONATA
MOROCCO

PLAYS BY ALLAN HAVIS, VOLUME TWO
A DARING BRIDE
THE LADIES OF FISHER COVE
SAINTE SIMONE

PLAYS BY TONY KUSHNER
A BRIGHT ROOM CALLED DAY
THE ILLUSION
SLAVS!

PLAYS BY RICHARD NELSON
EARLY PLAYS VOLUME ONE
CONJURING AN EVENT
JUNGLE COUP
THE KILLING OF YABLONSKI
SCOOPING

PLAYS BY RICHARD NELSON
EARLY PLAYS VOLUME TWO
BAL
THE RETURN OF PINOCCHIO
THE VIENNA NOTES

PLAYS BY RICHARD NELSON
EARLY PLAYS VOLUME THREE
AN AMERICAN COMEDY
JITTERBUGGING: SCENES OF SEX IN A NEW SOCIETY
RIP VAN WINKLE, OR "THE WORKS"

PLAYS BY LOUIS PHILLIPS
BONE THE SPEED
CARWASH
CONRAD ON THE VINE
ETHIOPIA
THE MAN WHO ATE EINSTEIN'S BRAIN
PRECISION MACHINES

PLAYS BY AISHAH RAHMAN
THE MOJO AND THE SAYSO
ONLY IN AMERICA
UNFINISHED WOMEN CRY IN NO MAN'S LAND WHILE A BIRD DIES
IN A GILDED CAGE

PLAYS BY EDWIN SÁNCHEZ
CLEAN
FLOOR SHOW: DOÑA SOL AND HER TRAINED DOG
TRAFFICKING IN BROKEN HEARTS

PLAYS BY NAOMI WALLACE
IN THE HEART OF AMERICA
SLAUGHTER CITY
THE WAR BOYS

BROADWAY PLAY PUBLISHING INC

TOP TEN BEST SELLING FULL-LENGTH PLAYS AND FULL-LENGTH PLAY COLLECTIONS

BATTERY

THE IMMIGRANT

NATIVE SPEECH

ONE FLEA SPARE

ON THE VERGE

PLAYS BY TONY KUSHNER
(CONTAINING A BRIGHT ROOM CALLED DAY,
THE ILLUSION, & SLAVS!)

PRELUDE TO A KISS

THE PROMISE

TALES OF THE LOST FORMICANS

TO GILLIAN ON HER 37TH BIRTHDAY